NINJA®
AIR FRYER
COOKBOOK FOR
BEGINNERS

NINJA

AIR FRYER

COOKBOOK FOR

BEGINNERS

75+ RECIPES FOR

FASTER, HEALTHIER & CRISPIER

FRIED FAVORITES

LINDA LARSEN

ROCKRIDGE
PRESS

———

For general information on our other products and services or to obtain technical support, please contact our Customer Care Department within the United States at (866) 744-2665, or outside the United States at (510) 253-0500.

———

Rockridge Press publishes its books in a variety of electronic and print formats. Some content that appears in print may not be available in electronic books, and vice versa.

———

TRADEMARKS: Rockridge Press and the Rockridge Press logo are trademarks or registered trademarks of Callisto Media Inc. and/or its affiliates, in the United States and other countries, and may not be used without written permission. All other trademarks are the property of their respective owners. Rockridge Press is not associated with any product or vendor mentioned in this book.

———

Interior and Cover Designer: Julie Schrader

Art Producer: Karen Beard

Editor: Salwa Jabado

Production Editor: Gleni Bartels

Photography: Photography: Copyright page: Cover and interior photography © 2019 Becky Stayner, food styling by Kathleen Phillips, except © Evi Abeler, pp.35, 54, 82, 107, 113, 129, 155, 168, 197; © Helene Dujardin, pp. 28, 41, 50, 63, 108, 130, 135, 136, 149, 172, 177; © Marija Vidal, pp. 22—23, 46—47, 150, 191; © Shutterstock, p. 66; © Darren Muir, p. 80. Author photo courtesy of Picture This Northfield.

ISBN: Print 978-1-64152-956-3 | eBook 978-1-64152-957-0

R1

———

I dedicate this book to my dear husband, Doug, my beautiful nieces Maddie and Grace, and my wonderful nephew Michael. They are a joy and a delight!

CONTENTS

INTRODUCTION

In my 30-year career as a home economist and cookbook author, I have used just about every appliance available to cook just about every type of food. And I have written about appliances from the slow cooker to microwaves to toaster ovens and pressure cookers. But I have not met an appliance with the versatility, efficiency, and ease of use the air fryer offers. The air fryer has been on the market for about 10 years. Many brands are available for purchase. But the best air fryer yet is the new Ninja® Air Fryer Max XL—it will transform how you feed your family.

With an air fryer on my counter, I no longer have to dig out my deep fryer when I want some sweet potato fries. I don't have to turn on my oven and heat up the house when I want a perfectly roasted chicken or baked cherry pie. And I don't have to spend lots of time cleaning because my stovetop is covered with grease that has even spilled onto the floor!

The air fryer is unique because it can fry, roast, bake, steam, stir-fry, cook, reheat, and even dehydrate foods with no hands-on work, all in one completely, and neatly, contained package. All you have to do is prepare the food, put it into the basket, turn the appliance on, and, occasionally, shake the basket for optimum crisping. The air fryer does the rest.

Many people are challenged by cooking at home, believing it is time-consuming, difficult, and messy. Home cooks can easily get into a rut by making the same recipes over and over. How many times have you stood at the refrigerator trying to decide how to cook those chicken breasts again? Or wondered how to make a meal in under an hour so you can sit down for a bit to recharge for the next day? That's why takeout restaurant meals and meal kits are so popular: they are easy and convenient and take little effort. But food from restaurants is typically very high in sodium and fat and is expensive; and, with meal kits, there's no opportunity to be creative in the kitchen.

Cooking your own food at home in an air fryer means you can control the ingredients and the nutrients they provide. You can add variety to your meals and have some fun unleashing your inner chef. Plus, you'll save money and time. Individual ingredients always cost less than prepared meals. The time savings can be significant: With these simple and flavorful recipes, you'll spend 10 to 15 minutes prepping ingredients and the air fryer does the rest—while you relax.

The new Ninja® Air Fryer Max XL takes air frying to the next level with a highest temperature setting of 450°F (Max Crisp). This temperature is best when cooking frozen foods: Frozen French fries, chicken patties, and breaded shrimp are so crisp and delicious when cooked on this Max Crisp setting.

And, unlike deep-frying, where you have to use cups of oil, when you use an air fryer you only need a spritz of oil to make super-crisp foods.

Seven programmable functions in Ninja Air Fryer Max XL means you don't have to guess about temperature and timing for foods such as chicken, fries, beef, and pork. Just press a button and the food will be juicy, crisp, and perfectly done, *every time.*

The larger-capacity basket that comes with the new Ninja Air Fryer Max XL lets you cook more food at the same time. That means if you are feeding more than two or three people, you won't have to cook in batches as you do with other air fryers. In the Ninja Air Fryer Max XL, your food will be crispier, will cook in less time, and will be delicious, every time.

And the best part? Cleanup is so simple. After the air fryer cools, just wipe down the inside and outside with a cloth. The air fryer basket and all accessories can go right into the dishwasher. Your counter stays clean, you will have used fewer utensils, and you can relax and enjoy time with your family instead of being tied to your kitchen.

In this book, you'll find recipes for everything from Mixed Berry Muffins (page 26) to Onion Rings (page 57). You'll serve perfectly cooked roast chicken, tender steak, hot and crispy pizza, and even doughnuts and cookies. We have even included "recipes" that aren't really recipes—they are tips and templates to help you make great food with ingredients you already have on hand. When you have a Ninja Air Fryer Max XL on your counter, you'll make recipes that are interesting, delicious, and good for you. And cooking, baking, frying, and roasting are easier than ever before.

1

Ninja® Air Fryer Max XL 101

The first air fryers were developed in 2010. Early models were simple, incorporating the heating element, fan, and basket with a few programmable functions and not a lot of versatility. As the market exploded, many companies introduced air fryers. Most were simple, with 3- or 4-quart baskets and just one or two cooking techniques or programmable functions.

The Ninja Air Fryer Max XL makes the leap from basic kitchen appliance to a superstar all-purpose kitchen champ. With this appliance on your kitchen counter, you can cook a steak for one or a roast chicken for four in just minutes with wonderful results. The Ninja Air Fryer Max XL is Ninja's hottest and fastest air fryer, which gives you more choices when roasting and air frying. The larger-capacity basket lets you easily feed six people in just one cooking session.

WHY THE NINJA AIR FRYER MAX XL?

The Ninja Air Fryer is the gold standard for air fryers on the market. And the new Ninja Air Fryer Max XL has enhanced controls, increased capacity, and higher temperatures to ensure you get perfect results every time.

Max Crisp Technology

The Ninja® Air Fryer Max XL has been developed to cook frozen foods, such as chicken nuggets and French fries, quickly and perfectly on the Max Crisp setting. When you push the "Max Crisp" button, the unit will heat to 450ºF. *You cannot adjust the temperature setting on this function*—to crisp to perfection requires this temperature. Always use the crisper plate when cooking with Max Crisp setting so the food is raised a bit off the bottom of the basket and air flows easily around the food for the crispest results.

7-in-1 programs

The 7-in-1 programs on the Ninja Air Fryer Max XL include Max Crisp, Air Fry, Air Roast, Air Broil, Bake, Reheat, and Dehydrate. You can adjust the cooking temperature for all these functions except Max Crisp, which heats only to 450ºF. These seven functions let you use the Max XL version as a substitute for a deep fryer, an oven, a broiler, a grill, and a dehydrator. All you do is press a button and the air fryer does the rest.

Up to 75 percent less fat than deep-frying

It's true: The air fryer makes delectable fried foods with 75 percent less fat than deep-frying, yet keeps the same texture. When deep-frying, the hot oil quickly removes moisture from the surface of the food, creating a crisp exterior, while the heat cooks the inside. But deep-fried food absorbs oil as it cooks, which explains why a baked potato has far fewer calories than its deep-fried French fry cousin made from that same potato.

Hot circulating air in an air fryer also removes moisture from the surface of the food just like deep-frying, but with very little oil, and produces a crisp crust and tender interior. The tiny amount of oil you use when air frying adds an insignificant number of calories to the dish. French fries from a whole potato made in an air fryer provide about 168 calories per serving, closer to that of a baked potato (which has 161 calories, according to the U.S. Department of Agriculture).

Faster cooking of frozen foods

Many frozen foods cook beautifully in the air fryer, usually faster than deep-frying, sautéing, or baking. You can add frozen veggies to the air fryer and they will be hot and tender in 10 to 15 minutes, versus 30 minutes in the oven. And frozen veggies roasted in the air fryer do not compare to microwaved vegetables, which can emerge soggy and limp, with cold spots because of uneven cooking.

Hotter temperatures

When roasting and deep-frying, hotter temperatures cook food more quickly and with less nutrient loss. Roasted chicken is burnished, browned, and juicy when cooked in the air fryer at 400°F. Roasted vegetables can be cooked at 400°F, too: They will be crisp outside and tender inside, with wonderful and flavorful caramelization. Frozen foods—from French fries to fritters and chicken nuggets to mozzarella sticks—will be the best you've ever tasted when cooked at 450°F on Max Crisp.

Easy to clean

The Ninja® Air Fryer Max XL is simple to clean. Unplug the appliance and wait for it to cool down, then remove the basket and any pans or racks and put them in the dishwasher or clean them in the sink using a nonabrasive sponge and some soap and water. The basket and racks are nonstick and so are easy to clean; any burned-on food will rinse off after a quick soak. Wipe down the inside and outside of the air fryer with a cloth and you're done!

How the Ninja Air Fryer Max XL Works

The Ninja Air Fryer Max XL is like a convection oven on steroids. The powerful heater and fan cook foods quickly and perfectly. The hot air circulates around the food, creating a crisp exterior while the interior cooks via conduction, that is, direct transfer of heat.

The cooking basket has slits on the bottom that let the heated air circulate all around the food, mimicking the deep-frying process. That means your chicken wings will be crisp all the way around and cooked evenly without using much oil at all. Most air fryer recipes use just a bit of oil for flavor, browning, and to keep bread crumbs intact.

Food browns in the air fryer because of what is known as the Maillard reaction. Carbohydrates, sugars, and proteins on the surface of food react with each other under high heat and dry conditions to produce the delicious fried-food taste and the desirable crispy crunchy brown crust.

The air fryer basket sits on a drip tray that collects any juices or fat released by the food during cooking. That means chicken breasts and roasted veggies will be crisp, even on the bottom, because the food isn't sitting in oil or juices as it cooks.

The programmable functions and temperature and time controls let you cook with just the touch of a button, eliminating guesswork.

NINJA® AIR FRYER MAX XL FEATURES

Your Ninja Air Fryer Max XL is an efficient machine with just a few moving parts. It is well engineered and designed to produce the best food with little effort on your part. You'll be more comfortable using the machine if you know the parts and understand how each works.

1. **Heating element:** The powerful heating element is a radiant heat source. It is placed above the food so you can broil as well as bake, air fry, and roast.

2. **Fan:** The fan on this unit is very powerful. It circulates air around the food so it cooks quickly and evenly and browns quickly, too.

3. **Fryer basket:** The ceramic-coated, nonstick, and PTFE- and PFOA-free basket holds the food as it cooks. The basket in the Max XL holds 5½ quarts, so you can cook more food and feed more people without having to cook in batches.

4. **Crisper plate:** This fits snugly inside the air fryer basket. It is also ceramic-coated, nonstick, and PTFE- and PFOA-free. The crisper plate is used when you want to raise food off the basket, which lets more air circulate around the food. It can be used with all functions except Air Roast.

5. **Electronic functions:** The Max XL has seven programmable functions. They are easy to use with just the push of a button. The functions include Max Crisp, Air Fry, Air Roast, Air Broil, Bake, Dehydrate, and Reheat.

6. **Timer:** The easily programmed timer is simple and accurate.

7. **Broil rack:** This rack holds foods closer to the heating element to give meals or sides a crispy, bubbly finish. This works great for cheese-topped dishes, steak, and salmon, especially.

Yes, You Can Air-Fry That

When most people think of air fryers, they think of crisp and crunchy French fries and savory, saucy chicken wings. Those foods do turn out beautifully in the air fryer, but this appliance is capable of so much more.

You can roast a big chunk of beef, bake a casserole or a quiche, and cook up a homemade pizza. Did you know you can make a frittata and an omelet in the air fryer? How about muffins, brownies, cookies, or cupcakes? You can roast a whole chicken, broil a steak, heat frozen food to crispy perfection, create a stir-fry or a creamy risotto, make homemade chips from all kinds of produce, and hardboil eggs in this wonderful appliance just by using the different cooking functions and temperatures.

The multiple functions of the Ninja® Air Fryer Max XL let you use the air fryer in place of the oven, microwave, and stovetop. You can bake, roast, fry, sauté, stir-fry, dehydrate, reheat, and steam just about any food. Instead of sautéing veggies in a pan on the stovetop, use the air fryer basket. There's no need to thaw frozen vegetables in the microwave oven; the air fryer will thaw and heat those ingredients perfectly.

And, before you know it, you will be creating your own recipes based on the recipes and tips in this book. The sky's the limit!

KNOW YOUR FUNCTIONS

These seven functions are unique to the Ninja Air Fryer Max XL unit. All you need to do is press the corresponding buttons and the unit will cook different foods perfectly. You just need to set the time.

Max Crisp

The Ninja Air Fryer Max XL has a new setting: Max Crisp! This setting cooks food at 450°F. You cannot change the temperature when you use this function. It is designed to make frozen foods super crisp, nicely browned, and perfectly reheated and tender on the inside. You no longer need to guess which temperature to use when cooking freezer staples such as French fries, chicken nuggets, and breaded shrimp, among other frozen foods.

Air Fry

This is the classic setting for air fryers that mimics deep-frying. It makes perfect French fries, chicken wings, and other typically deep-fried foods. The hot air circulates rapidly around the food, cooking it perfectly, creating a crisp, browned exterior. This function is different from a convection oven, as the fan speed is more powerful and the heat is contained in a smaller area. Don't be afraid to open the basket and check the food as it cooks. Because the air fryer heats so fast, the temperature quickly rebounds.

Air Broil

Broiling cooks foods with intense heat from one source only. Think of a broiler as an upside-down grill. Some foods, such as pork chops or ribs, can be cooked entirely with the Air Broil function. This function is used to finish a recipe and create a very crisp and nicely browned top. Broiling is also a great way to cook steaks or add a crisp crust to salmon fillets. If your food is done and you want it to have more of a browned crust, put the basket back into the air fryer and press broil. Within just a minute or two you'll have a perfectly crisp, browned crust on top of the food.

Dehydrate

Dehydrating foods is a great way to preserve them and a wonderful way to make healthy snacks. This function uses low heat and the fan to remove moisture from food. With the Dehydrate function, you can make crisp and tender chips from apples and pears, mangos, pineapple, sweet potatoes, kale and spinach, bananas, and beets. If you buy these types of snack foods from the store, they cost much more, and many contain chemicals and preservatives as well as extra sugar, salt, and fat. Dehydrating foods requires a long cooking time that can last several hours. But, because of the quiet fan setting on Dehydrate, you can dehydrate foods overnight while you sleep so they will be ready in the morning.

For best results with this function, dry foods before you dehydrate them. Slice or chop the food evenly so all pieces cook at the same rate. Trim off fat from meats before dehydrating. And put the food into the basket in an even, single layer; don't overlap food or it will dehydrate unevenly.

Air Roast

Roasting is a dry-heat cooking method that uses very high heat to sear the exterior of large cuts of beef and pork. It creates flavor through the Maillard reaction (see page 3) and also through caramelization, which is the oxidation of sugar molecules. Your air fryer cuts roasting times in half. Air fryer–roasted food is tender and juicy on the inside, with a wonderfully caramelized crisp and browned crust outside. And you don't need to do anything while the food cooks. The crisper plate is not used when cooking with this function.

Here's another advantage to using the air fryer to roast: You won't heat up your kitchen! You can prepare a beautiful beef roast on the hottest summer day and your kitchen will stay cool.

Bake

The air fryer is the perfect oven to bake everything from cookies to cheesecake to muffins, pies, crumbles, and fruit bars. With the Bake function, the air fryer becomes an efficient convection oven. Your baked goods are cooked in less time because the hot air circulates all around the food and creates a crisp, brown crust and tender interior. For example, the Marble Cheesecake (page 182) cooks in about 20 minutes, whereas a cheesecake baked in the oven takes close to an hour. Cookies, cakes, muffins, and breads will have a nice crust and a fluffy texture.

Reheat

Reheating foods is a snap with the Ninja® Air Fryer Max XL. If you've been dissatisfied with foods reheated in the microwave or toaster oven, you won't be disappointed with reheated foods in the air fryer. Put the cold food into the basket, press Reheat, and, in just a few minutes, your crisp air-fried foods will be just as mouthwatering and tasty as they were when you first made them—without being tough. You can reheat everything from pizza, fried chicken, and fish and chips to chicken patties, meatballs, soups, stews, and steak.

FREQUENTLY ASKED QUESTIONS

The answers to these frequently asked questions will help you use your Ninja Air Fryer and Ninja Air Fryer Max XL to their fullest capability. You can also refer to the Troubleshooting Guide included with your air fryer.

Can I stop the air fryer and shake or move food around during the cooking process?

Yes, you can! In fact, rearranging the food is encouraged whenever you use air fryers. Shaking the basket or rearranging the food using tongs lets you make sure that all the food cooks and browns evenly. The unit and timer will pause automatically when the basket is removed, and restart automatically when the basket is reinserted in the unit. Handle the air fryer basket carefully because it will be very hot; put it down on a heatproof surface such as a turned-off stovetop or a trivet.

Should I preheat the unit before I add food?

Yes. It only takes 3 minutes for the Ninja® Air Fryer and the Ninja Air Fryer Max XL to heat to cooking temperature. The basket must be in the unit and securely seated or the unit will not turn on. The basket will get quite hot during preheating, so the food starts cooking as soon as it is added. Handle the basket with care and never put it on a nonheatproof surface.

Can I convert conventional recipes to use in the air fryer?

Definitely. That's when cooking is fun! Just remember you should always reduce the cooking temperature by 25°F and reduce the cooking time by about 30 percent from conventional recipes, because the hot air circulating around the food speeds up the cooking process. Always check your food a few minutes before the timer goes off, as it's easy to add more time to get the best results, but you can't fix overcooked or burned foods. However, don't use recipes where the food is coated with a liquid batter because the batter will drip off the foods and make a mess before it sets.

How much oil should I add to the foods for best results?

Follow the recipes included in this cookbook and in your air fryer instruction booklet. They may call for tossing the food in about 1 tablespoon of oil before cooking. If you are cooking a recipe written for conventional cooking, use 2 to 3 teaspoons of oil and either toss the food with the oil or spritz it on using an oil mister. Make sure the food is evenly coated before cooking and never use so much oil that it drips off the food.

Why is my air fryer emitting smoke?

Smoke may come out of the air vents on the back of the unit during the cooking process. The color of the smoke will let you know what's going on inside. White smoke is completely normal and may actually be steam. If you see a lot of white smoke, the oil pan should be emptied and cleaned. Black smoke, however, indicates there is a problem. If you see black smoke, turn the air fryer off, unplug it, let the unit cool, remove the food, and take the air fryer to a service center.

Why isn't my food browning?

There are several reasons your food did not brown. For instance, it may have been too wet; always pat foods dry before adding them to the basket. The food may have been cooked on a temperature setting that was too low; in this case, put the basket back into the unit and turn the temperature up by 25°F, then cook the food for 2 to 3 minutes longer until it is nicely browned. Or the basket may have been over-crowded with too much food, which will require batch cooking. In this situation, remove half of the food and air fry until browned. Take the food out and add the remaining food, cooking it until browned. Then, return all the food to the basket and cook for another minute so everything is hot.

How do I pause the cooking time?

The unit will automatically stop the cooking time as soon as you remove the basket from the unit. You can change the cooking time by pressing the Up
and Down buttons on the unit's control panel. If you press Start/Stop during cooking, the timer will reset to HH:MM.

MODIFY RECIPES FOR THE ORIGINAL NINJA® AIR FRYER

All of the recipes throughout this cookbook were developed using the Ninja Air Fryer Max XL (model AF160), which has new and improved functionality: Bake, Air Broil, and Max Crisp, however most of the recipes throughout the book will work across all of the Ninja Air Fryer models. Follow my recommendations below for how to modify the recipes based on the Ninja Air Fryer you have!

Ninja Air Fryer Functions

Ninja Air Fryer (AF100)	Ninja Air Fryer Max XL (AF160)
Air Fry	Air Fry
Roast	Air Roast
Dehydrate	Dehydrate
Reheat	Reheat
	Bake
	Air Broil
	Max Crisp

BAKE: If you have a Ninja Air Fryer (AF100), you can modify the recipes throughout this cookbook that call for the Bake setting, which is only available in the Ninja Air Fryer Max XL (AF160). When a recipe calls for Bake, set the Ninja Air Fryer to Roast. However, note that the recipes may require a bit less cook time, as the convection fan operates at a lower speed on the Bake setting versus the Roast setting. For best results, check progress throughout cooking.

AIR BROIL: If you have a Ninja Air Fryer (AF100), you can modify the recipes throughout this cookbook that call for the Air Broil setting, which is only available in the Ninja Air Fryer Max XL (AF160). When a recipe calls for Air Broil, set the Ninja Air Fryer to Air Fry on the highest temperature setting instead. However, note that the Air Fry temperature will not get as hot as the Ninja Air Fryer Max XL Air Broil setting which goes up to 450°F.

MAX CRISP: The Max Crisp setting is only available on the Ninja Air Fryer Max XL (AF160) and is not used as a setting throughout this cookbook. The Max Crisp setting is used to crisp frozen foods to perfection. For a chart on how best to cook frozen foods in the Ninja Air Fryer, see page 206.

2

Start Crisping!

Let's get started with the Ninja® Air Fryer Max XL. Before using your air fryer for the first time, read the instruction manual and wipe down the inside and outside of the main unit before you start cooking. Wash the basket and crisper plate in soapy hot water, rinse, and dry. Put the air fryer on a stable surface near a wall outlet, making sure you leave about 5 inches of space between the wall and the back of the appliance for ventilation. Never use an extension cord with this appliance.

Read a recipe or two all the way through. Plug in your air fryer and get ready to enjoy fabulous foods. You can use your air fryer from morning to night to make everything from breakfast tarts to empanadas, steamed salmon, beef stir-fry, roasted potatoes, and fruit crumbles.

Collect the ingredients you'll need for each recipe and prep them. For most recipes, you'll need to peel and chop a few ingredients, collect some seasonings, and start cooking. Prep time is minimal when you use your air fryer because you are cooking with whole foods.

GETTING YOUR KITCHEN READY

One of the wonderful things about the Ninja Air Fryer Max XL is that you don't need a full kitchen to cook delicious meals. You do, however, need a refrigerator and some pantry staples to get the most out of this appliance. The recipes in this book do not call for any unusual or hard-to-obtain ingredients. You'll be able to shop at ordinary grocery or big box stores to make all the recipes in this book.

There are just a few tools and accessories you may want to buy to make using your air fryer as easy as possible.

Super-Simple Tools

For best results, you'll need a few tools to start cooking with your air fryer. One is a nice pair of spring-loaded silicone-tipped tongs to rearrange the food during cooking and to remove the food when it's done. A good, reliable food thermometer will let you know when foods are cooked to a safe temperature. And an oil mister to coat foods with just a bit of oil before cooking is indispensable. (There are dedicated oil misters on the market, but you can also use a food-safe spray bottle.)

Super-Simple Accessories

You may want to buy some helpful accessories, such as a small pan to cook cakes, a muffin pan, a pizza pan, a hardboiled egg insert, perforated paper liners, metal and bamboo skewers, a grill pan, a Bundt cake pan, or a mandoline so you can make super-thin slices of veggies. These fun accessories will expand your repertoire and make cooking with your air fryer more enjoyable.

Super-Simple Staples

Every cook has a different list of staples they like to keep on hand to make cooking easier and more enjoyable. These are the staples used most frequently in this book:

Butter: Nothing can replicate the rich flavor of butter. We don't use much butter in these recipes, but you'll want to keep some on hand, both salted and unsalted.

Milk: You can choose to buy cow's milk or branch out into plant-based milks, including almond milk, soy milk, coconut milk, and flax milk, depending on your dietary requirements.

Bread crumbs: This essential air-frying staple comes in several forms and flavors. Regular dried bread crumbs are perfect for many recipes, but you may want to try a specific type called panko bread crumbs. These crumbs have sharp edges for the crispiest results. (You can also make your own with any day-old bread or leftover croutons you might have in your pantry; just pulse them in a food processor until you reach the desired texture.)

Eggs: Eggs are used in many baked goods and are also used to make a crisp crust. Choose large Grade A eggs and keep them refrigerated.

Flour: Flour is used to make a good coating on air-fried foods and in cake, cookie, muffin, and brownie batters. Store all-purpose and whole-wheat flours in your pantry.

Mustard and ketchup: These condiments can be used as dipping sauces and add great flavor when used to coat meats before they are breaded.

Fruits and vegetables: Keep potatoes, onions, garlic, apples, pears, and leafy greens on hand to make delicious and healthy meals.

Super-Simple Spice Rack

Herbs and spices are essential to good cooking. Label the spices you buy and discard them after a year, as they lose flavor over time.

Salt and pepper: Every dish, even dessert, needs some salt. Different kinds of salts have different densities; I suggest coarse kosher salt. Buy black, white, and cayenne pepper to keep in your spice rack as well.

Dried thyme: This herb has a lemony, woodsy flavor that pairs well with vegetables, fish, and chicken.

Dried basil: Basil is used in Italian cooking. It has a minty and lemony flavor and is used with chicken, pork, and fish.

Garlic and onion powders: These spices are a great substitute for fresh minced garlic and onion, which can burn in the air fryer.

Chili powder: This spice blend comes in many different heat levels, from mild to super spicy; it's delicious in Mexican-style dishes. Choose your favorite to keep on hand.

Curry powder: This spice is a blend of many spices, including cinnamon, turmeric, ginger, mustard, cardamom, and pepper. It's often used in Indian cooking.

Dry mustard: This intense form of mustard is great for coating foods and adding flavor to casseroles.

Cinnamon: Cinnamon is used in many baked goods and adds a sweet, woodsy aroma.

Red pepper flakes: This spicy addition to the spice rack adds heat to many recipes.

Paprika: This spice is used to add color to coatings, to infuse foods with a rich flavor, and to sprinkle on casseroles. You can buy sweet or smoked paprika.

Dried Italian seasoning: This combination of herbs is perfect for Italian dishes. It is made from dried basil, oregano, marjoram, rosemary, and thyme.

STEP-BY-STEP AIR FRYING

Although it is very easy to use the air fryer, there are some steps to follow for best results.

1. First, read the recipe entirely and make sure you understand the instructions and the steps. Collect all the ingredients needed and any measuring spoons or cups.

2. If a recipe calls for spraying the cooking basket with a bit of oil, do so before preheating the air fryer.

3. If cooking a food high in fat, add some water to the drip pan to reduce smoke.

4. Plug in the air fryer, slide in the basket, and preheat it according to the instructions. Preheating takes about 3 minutes. The temperature for each recipe will vary depending on the type of food you're cooking. If you're following a conventional recipe, reduce the temperature by 25ºF, or choose one of the programmable cooking times.

5. Peel, chop, cube, mix, bread, and combine ingredients as directed in the recipe. Most foods are tossed or sprayed with a little oil to keep bread crumbs attached, or to add flavor or color. If you are breading food, press the bread crumbs on so they adhere and stay on the food during air frying.

6. Place the food in the air fryer basket. **Be careful—the basket is hot!** Don't set the air fryer basket directly on the counter; put it on a trivet or hot pad. Don't crowd the food, or it may not brown evenly. Be sure to shake the basket for the best crisping.

7. If you do layer food, turn the food with silicone-tipped tongs halfway through the cooking time to ensure even browning. When cooking foods such as fries, shake the basket often for even browning and cooking.

8. Let the air fryer work. This is a good time to do the minimal cleanup from preparing the ingredients.

9. If making a recipe for the first time, check for doneness a few minutes before the cook time specified in the recipe ends. You can always cook foods longer, but it's impossible to rescue overcooked food.

10. Check to see that the food is done. Most recipes suggest doneness tests, such as a browned crust or cakes that spring back when lightly touched in the center. Meats, poultry, seafood, and egg dishes should be checked with a food thermometer to make sure they are cooked to a safe temperature.

   - **Beef** (not ground) should be cooked to 145ºF.
   - **Chicken** (including ground chicken and ground turkey) should be cooked to 165ºF.
   - **Egg** dishes should be cooked to 160ºF.
   - **Fish** should be cooked to 145ºF.
   - **Ground meats, such as beef, pork, veal, and lamb,** should be cooked to 160ºF.
   - **Whole cuts of pork** are safe when cooked to 145ºF, with a 3-minute resting time, but ribs should be cooked to 190ºF to melt the collagen so they are tender.

11. Use silicone-tipped tongs to remove the finished food from the air fryer basket. Never tip the basket over a plate or bowl to remove the food; oil or hot liquid in the drip pan under the basket could spill out, ruining the food or burning your hands.

12. Put the basket back into the air fryer, turn it off, unplug it, and let the appliance cool while you eat. When your meal is complete, simply clean the basket and wipe down the air fryer!

No Recipe? No Problem

There are times you may have ingredients to use but no recipe or time to find one. Never fear! Here are some instructions for simple, delicious combinations that will put a meal on the table in minutes. Also, be sure to check out the Air Fry Cooking Charts and Dehydrate Charts starting on page 204 for other ingredient preparations and air fryer times.

RECIPE	INGREDIENTS	TEMPERATURE	TIME	DIRECTIONS
Beef kebabs	Cubed sirloin tip or top round steak Whole mushrooms Bell pepper slices Yellow summer squash Your favorite barbecue sauce or marinade Salt and pepper	390°F	10 to 14 minutes	Wash the mushrooms; slice the bell pepper and summer squash. You can use any veggie you'd like. Thread the veggies and beef onto 6-inch skewers. Brush with the barbecue sauce, season with salt and pepper, and air fry, turning once, until the beef reaches 145°F.
Roast chicken	1 (4-pound) roasting chicken Olive oil Salt and pepper Dried thyme, basil, or marjoram Lemon or orange	350°F	50 to 60 minutes	Make sure the chicken will fit into the basket. Do not rinse the chicken. Pat dry and brush with a bit of olive oil. Sprinkle with salt and pepper and any seasonings you'd like. Slice the lemon or orange and put it into the cavity. Place the chicken in the air fryer basket and roast until the chicken reaches 165°F.

RECIPE	INGREDIENTS	TEMPERATURE	TIME	DIRECTIONS
French bread pizza	½ loaf French bread Pizza or tomato sauce Grated cheese, such as mozzarella Mushroom slices or bell pepper pieces Sliced pepperoni or other cooked meat	400°F	4 to 5 minutes	Halve the French bread lengthwise; cut the halves into four (4-inch) sections. Top with pizza sauce, cheese, and any veggies and/or cooked meats. Air fry until the pizzas are hot and the cheese melts.
Frittata	1 tablespoon butter About ½ cup chopped vegetables, such as onion, bell pepper, or asparagus 5 eggs 2 tablespoons milk Salt and pepper 1 cup grated cheese, such as Cheddar, Colby, or Swiss	360°F	15 to 25 minutes	In a 6-inch round pan, combine the butter and veggies. Air fry for 5 minutes. In a medium bowl, beat the eggs with the milk, salt, and pepper. Pour over the vegetables in the pan. Set the pan into the air fryer basket and air fry for 5 to 7 minutes until the eggs are set. Sprinkle with the cheese and air fry for 1 minute more until the cheese melts.
Chicken fingers	Chicken tenderloins Oil or mustard Grated Parmesan cheese Bread crumbs Spices, such as garlic and onion powder	390°F	5 to 7 minutes	Halve the tenderloins crosswise. Brush with a bit of oil or mustard and coat in the cheese, crumbs, and spices. Air fry, flipping once, until the chicken reaches 165°F.

RECIPE	INGREDIENTS	TEMPERATURE	TIME	DIRECTIONS
Veggie fries	Carrots Green beans Zucchini Oil Regular or panko bread crumbs Seasonings, such as Italian seasoning Grated Parmesan cheese (optional) Salt and pepper	400°F	7 to 12 minutes	Slice the veggies into thin sticks so they look like fries. Toss the bread crumbs with a bit of oil and seasonings, if you'd like. Roll the veggie sticks in this mixture, pressing the breading onto the food. Air fry, shaking the basket once, until the veggies are crisp and tender. Season with salt and pepper.
Baked potato	3 or 4 medium (6-ounce) russet potatoes 2 teaspoons oil or melted butter Salt and pepper	400°F	30 to 40 minutes	Scrub the potatoes and pat dry. Prick each with a fork 5 times and put into the basket. Air roast for 20 minutes, brush with oil or butter, and continue cooking for 10 to 20 minutes more, or until the potato reaches about 200°F in the center. Slit the potato and season with salt and pepper. Serve with sour cream, cheese, salsa, taco sauce, cooked chicken, or cooked sausage.

7 TIPS FOR THE PERFECT CRISP

The Ninja® Air Fryer Max XL is simple to use. You'll have success no matter what you cook in it, especially if you use the preprogrammed functions. But, for best results every time, follow these tips for the perfect crisp finish and tender texture.

1. **Preheat the air fryer for about 3 minutes before you add the food.** That way, cooking starts immediately and the food will have the best crisp and brown crust. You'll hear the sizzle as you (carefully) add the food to the basket. Use this preheat time to prepare the ingredients.

2. **Spray the fryer basket and any pans with oil before you add the food.** Use an oil mister for even coating. Choose an oil with a high smoke point (the temperature when the oil breaks down and starts to smoke). Those oils include extra-virgin olive oil at 405°F, peanut at 440°F, sesame and corn at 450°F, sunflower at 480°F, safflower at 510°F, and avocado at 520°F. Avoid regular olive oil because of its lower smoke point, and don't use salted butter, because foods will stick. Avoid commercial non-stick baking sprays because they can react with the ceramic coating and make the basket more vulnerable to chipping. Anywhere in this book that it says "cooking oil spray," it refers to oil in an oil mister, not to any commercial product.

3. **Don't cook foods coated with a liquid or runny batter.** When you put battered foods into oil, the batter firms on contact. But, in an air fryer, it takes about 1 minute for the batter to dehydrate and become firm, so it can drip off the food and make a mess. Use foods coated with bread crumbs or cheese or a combination. You can also make an excellent crust by dipping the food into flour, then beaten egg, then into flour again, or bread crumbs. Press the crumbs onto the food and it's ready to cook.

4. **Coat most food with a little bit of oil before it cooks.** That oil will sizzle in the air fryer's heat, mimicking deep-frying without all the fat. The fat also ensures the food browns evenly. It also helps bread crumbs stick to the food, so they won't drop off or go flying around in the moving air.

5. **Give the food space in the air fryer.** If you crowd food in the basket, it won't brown and crisp evenly. You can get around this rule if you shake the basket several times during cooking. But, for best results, leave about ¼ inch of space around each piece of food.

6. **Move the food around!** Remove the air fryer basket and shake small items, such as chicken wings or veggie fries, a couple of times during the cooking process. This helps ensure that every piece has a brown, crisp coating and that the food cooks evenly. Flip steaks or chicken breasts halfway through the cooking time so they brown well on both sides. Don't worry about the temperature dropping while the basket is out of the air fryer; it reheats immediately.

7. **Clean your air fryer after every use.** Drippings in the basket must be removed or the next batch of food may taste and smell like the batch cooked before it. A dirty air fryer may also start to smoke, which will ruin the taste of the food and may damage the appliance or your kitchen. And any oil or grease left in the air cooker can become rancid, which will ruin your next batch of food. Remember that cleanup is easy and only takes a few minutes.

ABOUT THE RECIPES

All recipes in this book stand out for their ease of preparation, use of all the attributes of the Ninja® Air Fryer Max XL, speed, and, of course, superb texture and taste. Each recipe is labeled with a few defining words, including Dairy Free, Family Friendly, Fast, Gluten Free, Nut Free, and Vegetarian or Vegan. Fast recipes can be ready to eat in 30 minutes or less, start to finish. Family-Friendly recipes will serve at least four people and use kid-friendly ingredients. Some of the recipes will mimic deep-fried favorites, whereas others use the air fryer to bake, stir-fry, roast, and steam.

Most recipes include some substitutions for ingredients based on dietary restrictions. For instance, if you can't eat gluten, a recipe developed with wheat pasta will include a tip to make the recipe gluten-free. Or, if you can't find an ingredient, the recipe will give you alternatives to use instead.

The recipes encompass all the meals you eat during the day. Breakfast choices are quick to prepare and will tempt appetites early in the morning. Snacks and appetizers are great for a mid-afternoon treat and can be served when you entertain. Vegetables and sides round out a meal and are great when you want to grill some salmon or a steak and need a healthy dish on the side. Fish and seafood cook beautifully in the air fryer; fish fillets come out tender and moist, with a wonderfully crisp crust. Poultry is one of the best foods to cook in the air fryer; chicken breasts stay moist and juicy. Beef, pork, and lamb are great choices for this appliance, too; you can cook everything from a steak to pork chops to a beef roast in the Ninja® Air Fryer Max XL. And who could forget dessert? These sublime recipes will end your meal on a satisfying note.

The recipes make the most of the Ninja Air Fryer Max XL's versatile cooking functions, including Air Fry, Air Roast, Air Broil, Dehydrate, Bake, and Reheat. Only a few recipes have sauces or glazes prepared on the stovetop or in the microwave. The air fryer will do most of the cooking!

Once comfortable with the air fryer, you can change some of the recipes to make them your own. Use the "No Recipe? No Problem" chart (page 16), and the Air Fry Cooking Charts and Dehydrate Charts (starting on page 204) to help you create your own masterpieces. You'll see that you can prepare the foods you want to eat, make them healthier, cook in less time, and have much less cleanup. You will spend less money on your food budget, enjoy healthier recipes with less fat, spend less time in the kitchen on cooking and cleanup, and become more confident and creative in the kitchen.

Scale It Up

The recipes in this cookbook were developed using the original Ninja® Air Fryer, which has a 4-quart basket. But never fear: Most of the recipes will work with newer Ninja Air Fryer models. If you have the Ninja® Foodi® 6-in-1 8-quart 2-Basket Air Fryer, you can easily modify the recipes throughout this book—plus you can scale the recipes up to feed more people! The Foodi 2-Basket Air Fryer has two 4-quart air fry baskets which allow you to air fry twice the amount of food for bigger family-sized meals. Note that some of the recipes may require an extra shake of the crisping basket. For best results, check progress throughout cooking, and shake the basket frequently. As a good rule of thumb, you can double Air Fry recipes like french fries and chicken nuggets when using the 2-Basket Air Fryer. In addition, the DualZone™ Technology features the Smart Finish feature—to cook two foods two ways, finishing at the same time—and a Match Cook button to easily copy settings across zones for full 8-quart capacity. This allows you to have a complete meal without one food finishing before another.

Blueberry Breakfast
Cobbler, page 24

3

Breakfast

Blueberry Breakfast Cobbler

PREP TIME: 5 MINUTES / COOK TIME: 15 MINUTES / SERVES 4 / 350°F / BAKE

A cobbler for breakfast is a wonderful treat. When you use the air fryer, this recipe is quick enough to make even on busy weekday mornings. Use your favorite granola to top the sweet and juicy blueberries or try your own homemade Granola (page 25).

⅓ cup whole-wheat pastry flour

¾ teaspoon baking powder

Dash sea salt

½ cup 2% milk

2 tablespoons pure maple syrup

½ teaspoon vanilla extract

Cooking oil spray

½ cup fresh blueberries

¼ cup Granola (page 25), or plain store-bought granola

FAST, FAMILY FAVORITE, VEGETARIAN

VARIATION TIP: You can make this easy and decadent recipe with other fruits if you'd like. Try a mix of raspberries and sliced strawberries or add blackberries to the blueberries. Any combination of berries is delicious. Or, change the fruit completely based on what's in season.

1. In a medium bowl, whisk the flour, baking powder, and salt. Add the milk, maple syrup, and vanilla and gently whisk, just until thoroughly combined.

2. Preheat the unit by selecting BAKE, setting the temperature to 350°F, and setting the time to 3 minutes. Select START/STOP to begin.

3. Spray a 6-by-2-inch round baking pan with cooking oil and pour the batter into the pan. Top evenly with the blueberries and granola.

4. Once the unit is preheated, place the pan into the basket.

5. Select BAKE, set the temperature to 350°F, and set the time to 15 minutes. Select START/STOP to begin.

6. When the cooking is complete, the cobbler should be nicely browned and a knife inserted into the middle should come out clean. Enjoy plain or topped with a little vanilla yogurt.

Per Serving: Calories: 112; Total fat: 1g; Saturated fat: <1g; Cholesterol: 3mg; Sodium: 69mg; Carbohydrates: 23g; Fiber: 2g; Protein: 3g

Granola

PREP TIME: 5 MINUTES / COOK TIME: 40 MINUTES / MAKES 2 CUPS / 250°F / BAKE

Granola is a great recipe for the air fryer. This cereal is so delicious when you make it yourself—you'll never buy a boxed version again. And you'll know exactly what was used to make the cereal you feed your family.

1 cup rolled oats

3 tablespoons pure maple syrup

1 tablespoon sugar

1 tablespoon neutral-flavored oil, such as refined coconut, sunflower, or safflower

¼ teaspoon sea salt

¼ teaspoon ground cinnamon

¼ teaspoon vanilla extract

DAIRY FREE, FAMILY FAVORITE, GLUTEN FREE, NUT FREE, VEGAN

VARIATION TIP: You can change this recipe to include some of your favorite granola ingredients, such as dried fruits, different types of nuts, and even goodies such as chocolate chips. Stir them in after the granola is done, but before it's completely cool.

1. Insert the crisper plate into the basket and the basket into the unit. Preheat the unit by selecting BAKE, setting the temperature to 250°F, and setting the time to 3 minutes. Select START/STOP to begin.

2. In a medium bowl, stir together the oats, maple syrup, sugar, oil, salt, cinnamon, and vanilla until thoroughly combined. Transfer the granola to a 6-by-2-inch round baking pan.

3. Once the unit is preheated, place the pan into the basket.

4. Select BAKE, set the temperature to 250°F and set the time to 40 minutes. Select START/STOP to begin.

5. After 10 minutes, stir the granola well. Resume cooking, stirring the granola every 10 minutes, for a total of 40 minutes, or until the granola is lightly browned and mostly dry.

6. When the cooking is complete, place the granola on a plate to cool. It will become crisp as it cools. Store the completely cooled granola in an airtight container in a cool, dry place for 1 to 2 weeks.

Per Serving (½ cup): Calories: 165; Total fat: 5g; Saturated fat: 1g; Cholesterol: 0mg; Sodium: 120mg; Carbohydrates: 27g; Fiber: 2g; Protein: 3g

Mixed Berry Muffins

This easy recipe makes eight light and tender muffins your entire family will love. Choose your favorite fresh berries: chopped strawberries, blueberries, and raspberries are all delicious.

1⅓ cups plus 1 tablespoon all-purpose flour, divided

¼ cup granulated sugar

2 tablespoons light brown sugar

2 teaspoons baking powder

2 eggs

⅔ cup whole milk

⅓ cup safflower oil

1 cup mixed fresh berries

FAMILY FAVORITE, NUT FREE, VEGETARIAN

1. In a medium bowl, stir together 1⅓ cups of flour, the granulated sugar, brown sugar, and baking powder until mixed well.

2. In a small bowl, whisk the eggs, milk, and oil until combined. Stir the egg mixture into the dry ingredients just until combined.

3. In another small bowl, toss the mixed berries with the remaining 1 tablespoon of flour until coated. Gently stir the berries into the batter.

4. Double up 16 foil muffin cups to make 8 cups.

5. Insert the crisper plate into the basket and the basket into the unit. Preheat the unit by selecting BAKE, setting the temperature to 315°F, and setting the time to 3 minutes. Select START/STOP to begin.

6. Once the unit is preheated, place 4 cups into the basket and fill each three-quarters full with the batter.

7. Select BAKE, set the temperature to 315°F, and set the time for 17 minutes. Select START/STOP to begin.

8. After about 12 minutes, check the muffins. If they spring back when lightly touched with your finger, they are done. If not, resume cooking.

9. When the cooking is done, transfer the muffins to a wire rack to cool.

10. Repeat steps 6, 7, and 8 with the remaining muffin cups and batter.

11. Let the muffins cool for 10 minutes before serving.

Per Serving: *Calories: 230; Total fat: 11g; Saturated fat: 2g; Cholesterol: 43mg; Sodium: 26mg; Carbohydrates: 30g; Fiber: 1g; Protein: 4g*

INGREDIENT TIP: You can use frozen berries in this recipe, but don't thaw them before use. If frozen berries are thawed before they are added to batter, they will make the batter too wet, and the berries may turn the muffins an unusual color.

Homemade Strawberry Breakfast Tarts

PREP TIME: 15 MINUTES / COOK TIME: 10 MINUTES PER BATCH / SERVES 6 / 375°F / BAKE

These kid-friendly breakfast tarts also make a wonderful breakfast treat for adults! The crispy crust paired with the warm, sweet-tart filling feels like the ultimate indulgence. For a less sweet version, omit the frosting. Either way, once you make your own homemade breakfast tarts, you will never revert to store-bought again.

2 refrigerated piecrusts

½ cup strawberry preserves

1 teaspoon cornstarch

Cooking oil spray

½ cup low-fat vanilla yogurt

1 ounce cream cheese, at room temperature

3 tablespoons confectioners' sugar

Rainbow sprinkles, for decorating

FAMILY FAVORITE, NUT FREE, VEGETARIAN

1. Place the piecrusts on a flat surface. Using a knife or pizza cutter, cut each piecrust into 3 rectangles, for 6 total. Discard any unused dough from the piecrust edges.

2. In a small bowl, stir together the preserves and cornstarch. Mix well, ensuring there are no lumps of cornstarch remaining.

3. Scoop 1 tablespoon of the strawberry mixture onto the top half of each piece of piecrust.

4. Fold the bottom of each piece up to enclose the filling. Using the back of a fork, press along the edges of each tart to seal.

5. Insert the crisper plate into the basket and the basket into the unit. Preheat the unit by selecting BAKE, setting the temperature to 375ºF, and setting the time to 3 minutes. Select START/STOP to begin.

6. Once the unit is preheated, spray the crisper plate with cooking oil. Working in batches, spray the breakfast tarts with cooking oil and place them into the basket in a single layer. Do not stack the tarts.

(continued)

Homemade Strawberry Breakfast Tarts   *continued*

7. Select BAKE, set the temperature to 375ºF, and set the time to 10 minutes. Select START/STOP to begin.

8. When the cooking is complete, the tarts should be light golden brown. Let the breakfast tarts cool fully before removing them from the basket.

9. Repeat steps 5, 6, 7, and 8 for the remaining breakfast tarts.

10. In a small bowl, stir together the yogurt, cream cheese, and confectioners' sugar. Spread the breakfast tarts with the frosting and top with sprinkles.

COOKING TIP: Check on the tarts after 7 or 8 minutes to ensure they are not too crisp. For softer breakfast tarts, allow them to cook until they turn light brown. For crispier tarts, cook until they are golden brown.

Per Serving: *Calories: 408; Total fat: 20.5g; Saturated fat: 9g; Cholesterol: 6mg; Sodium: 400mg; Carbohydrates: 56g; Fiber: 0g; Protein: 1g*

Everything Bagels

PREP TIME: 10 MINUTES / COOK TIME: 10 MINUTES / MAKES 2 BAGELS / 330°F / BAKE

Who knew that making homemade bagels could be so easy? With only a handful of ingredients, these Everything Bagels are the perfect way to start the day. Make enough for a single morning or double your batch and have enough for the whole weekend. There's an everything bagel spice mix available in some supermarkets and online, or make your own (see Tip).

½ **cup self-rising flour, plus more for dusting**

½ **cup plain Greek yogurt**

1 egg

1 tablespoon water

4 teaspoons everything bagel spice mix

Cooking oil spray

1 tablespoon butter, melted

DAIRY FREE, FAMILY FAVORITE, FAST, VEGETARIAN

1. In a large bowl, using a wooden spoon, stir together the flour and yogurt until a tacky dough forms. Transfer the dough to a lightly floured work surface and roll the dough into a ball.

2. Cut the dough into 2 pieces and roll each piece into a log. Form each log into a bagel shape, pinching the ends together.

3. In a small bowl, whisk the egg and water. Brush the egg wash on the bagels.

4. Sprinkle 2 teaspoons of the spice mix on each bagel and gently press it into the dough.

5. Insert the crisper plate into the basket and the basket into the unit. Preheat the unit by selecting BAKE, setting the temperature to 330°F, and setting the time to 3 minutes. Select START/STOP to begin.

6. Once the unit is preheated, spray the crisper plate with cooking spray. Drizzle the bagels with the butter and place them into the basket.

(continued)

Everything Bagels *continued*

7. Select BAKE, set the temperature to 330°F, and set the time to 10 minutes. Select START/STOP to begin.

8. When the cooking is complete, the bagels should be lightly golden on the outside. Serve warm.

Per Serving *(1 bagel): Calories: 271; Total fat: 13g; Saturated fat: 6g; Cholesterol: 117mg; Sodium: 803mg; Carbohydrates: 28g; Fiber: 1g; Protein: 10g*

SUBSTITUTION TIP: You can make your own everything bagel spice mix. In an airtight container, combine 4 tablespoons sesame seeds, 3 tablespoons poppy seeds, 2 tablespoons dehydrated minced onion, 1 teaspoon garlic powder, and 1 teaspoon salt. Store at room temperature.

Easy Maple-Glazed Doughnuts

PREP TIME: 10 MINUTES / COOK TIME: 14 MINUTES / MAKES 8 DOUGHNUTS / 350°F / AIR FRY

Making doughnuts in your air fryer is definitely faster than running out to the corner doughnut shop. These Easy Maple-Glazed Doughnuts bake in just 5 minutes per batch, with no oil, and are so incredibly delicious—perfect for weekend mornings. When you are done, it is also fun to take all those extra pieces of dough you cut out and air fry them for 3 minutes to make doughnut holes.

1 (8-count) can jumbo flaky refrigerator biscuits

Cooking oil spray

½ cup light brown sugar

¼ cup butter

3 tablespoons milk

2 cups confectioners' sugar, plus more for dusting (optional)

2 teaspoons pure maple syrup

FAST, NUT FREE, VEGETARIAN

1. Insert the crisper plate into the basket and the basket into the unit. Preheat the unit by selecting AIR FRY, setting the temperature to 350°F, and setting the time to 3 minutes. Select START/STOP to begin.

2. Remove the biscuits from the tube and cut out the center of each biscuit with a small, round cookie cutter.

3. Once the unit is preheated, spray the crisper plate with cooking oil. Working in batches, place 4 doughnuts into the basket.

4. Select AIR FRY, set the temperature to 350°F, and set the time to 5 minutes. Select START/STOP to begin.

5. When the cooking is complete, place the doughnuts on a plate. Repeat steps 3 and 4 with the remaining doughnuts.

6. In a small saucepan over medium heat, combine the brown sugar, butter, and milk. Heat until the butter is melted and the sugar is dissolved, about 4 minutes.

(continued)

Easy Maple-Glazed Doughnuts *continued*

7. Remove the pan from the heat and whisk in the confectioners' sugar and maple syrup until smooth.

8. Dip the slightly cooled doughnuts into the maple glaze. Place them on a wire rack and dust with confectioners' sugar (if using). Let rest just until the glaze sets. Enjoy the doughnuts warm.

Per Serving *(1 doughnut): Calories: 219; Total fat: 10g; Saturated fat: 5g; Cholesterol: 16mg; Sodium: 362mg; Carbohydrates: 30g; Fiber: 0g; Protein: 2g*

VARIATION TIP: It's easy to make different kinds of glazes for your homemade doughnuts. For a chocolate glaze, omit the brown sugar and maple syrup and add 2 tablespoons cocoa powder. For a vanilla glaze, omit the brown sugar and maple syrup and add ½ teaspoon vanilla extract.

Chocolate-Filled Doughnut Holes

PREP TIME: 10 MINUTES / COOK TIME: 8 TO 12 MINUTES PER BATCH /
MAKES 24 DOUGHNUT HOLES / 330°F / AIR FRY

Doughnut holes are the little round puffs made from the center bit of dough that is removed when doughnuts are formed. In this case, you use biscuit dough and wrap each piece around a couple of chocolate chips. When baked, the chocolate inside melts, making a decadent breakfast treat.

1 (8-count) can refrigerated biscuits

Cooking oil spray

48 semisweet chocolate chips

3 tablespoons melted unsalted butter

¼ cup confectioners' sugar

FAMILY FAVORITE,
NUT FREE, VEGETARIAN

VARIATION TIP: Get creative with the fillings for these little treats. Use a combination of chocolate chips and nuts, or try chopped-up candy bars. Just make sure the dough isn't overfilled, or the doughnut holes may split during air frying.

1. Separate the biscuits and cut each biscuit into thirds, for 24 pieces.

2. Flatten each biscuit piece slightly and put 2 chocolate chips in the center. Wrap the dough around the chocolate and seal the edges well.

3. Insert the crisper plate into the basket and the basket into the unit. Preheat the unit by selecting AIR FRY, setting the temperature to 330ºF, and setting the time to 3 minutes. Select START/STOP to begin.

4. Once the unit is preheated, spray the crisper plate with cooking oil. Brush each doughnut hole with a bit of the butter and place it into the basket.Select AIR FRY, set the temperature to 330ºF, and set the time between 8 and 12 minutes. Select START/STOP to begin.

5. The doughnuts are done when they are golden brown. When the cooking is complete, place the doughnut holes on a plate and dust with the confectioners' sugar. Serve warm.

Per Serving: *Calories: 393; Total fat: 17g; Saturated fat: 8g; Cholesterol: 24mg; Sodium: 787mg; Carbohydrates: 55g; Fiber: 1g; Protein: 5g*

Classic Hash Browns

PREP TIME: 15 MINUTES / COOK TIME: 20 MINUTES / SERVES 4 / 360°F / AIR FRY

Making homemade hash browns is a cinch. All you need is a vegetable peeler and a cheese grater. These potatoes are crispy on the outside and fluffy on the inside.

4 russet potatoes, peeled
1 teaspoon paprika
Salt

Freshly ground black pepper
Cooking oil spray

FAMILY FAVORITE,
GLUTEN FREE, VEGAN

1. Using a box grater or food processor, shred the potatoes. If your grater has different hole sizes, use the largest holes.

2. Place the shredded potatoes in a large bowl of cold water. Let sit for 5 minutes. (Cold water helps remove excess starch from the potatoes.) Stir them to help dissolve the starch.

3. Insert the crisper plate into the basket and the basket into the unit. Preheat the unit by selecting AIR FRY, setting the temperature to 360°F, and setting the time to 3 minutes. Select START/STOP to begin.

4. Drain the potatoes and pat them with paper towels until the potatoes are completely dry. Season the potatoes with the paprika, salt, and pepper.

5. Once the unit is preheated, spray the crisper plate with cooking oil. Spray the potatoes with the cooking oil and place them into the basket.

6. Select AIR FRY, set the temperature to 360°F, and set the time to 20 minutes. Select START/STOP to begin.

(continued)

Classic Hash Browns *continued*

7. After 5 minutes, remove the basket and shake the potatoes. Reinsert the basket to resume cooking. Continue shaking the basket every 5 minutes (a total of 4 times) until the potatoes are done.

8. When the cooking is complete, remove the hash browns from the basket and serve warm.

Per Serving: Calories: 150; Total fat: 0g; Saturated fat: 0g; Cholesterol: 0mg; Sodium: 52mg; Carbohydrates: 34g; Fiber: 5g; Protein: 4g

SUBSTITUTION TIP: You can use other types of potatoes in this easy recipe. Yukon gold potatoes make buttery-tasting hash browns. Sweet potato hash browns are delicious, too, as are red potatoes. Just drain and dry the potatoes as thoroughly as possible before adding them to the air fryer.

Fried Chicken and Waffles

PREP TIME: 10 MINUTE / COOK TIME: 30 MINUTES / SERVES 4 / 400°F, THEN 360°F / AIR FRY

Fried chicken and waffles is a classic Southern breakfast. The combination of savory and crisp chicken with tender, sweet waffles is unmatched—don't knock it until you try it! Maple syrup drizzled over each serving makes a perfect finishing touch.

8 whole chicken wings

1 teaspoon garlic powder

Chicken seasoning, for preparing the chicken

Freshly ground black pepper

½ cup all-purpose flour

Cooking oil spray

8 frozen waffles

Pure maple syrup, for serving (optional)

FAMILY FAVORITE, NUT FREE

1. In a medium bowl, combine the chicken and garlic powder and season with chicken seasoning and pepper. Toss to coat.

2. Transfer the chicken to a resealable plastic bag and add the flour. Seal the bag and shake it to coat the chicken thoroughly.

3. Insert the crisper plate into the basket and the basket into the unit. Preheat the unit by selecting AIR FRY, setting the temperature to 400°F, and setting the time to 3 minutes. Select START/STOP to begin.

4. Once the unit is preheated, spray the crisper plate with cooking oil. Using tongs, transfer the chicken from the bag to the basket. It is okay to stack the chicken wings on top of each other. Spray them with cooking oil.

5. Select AIR FRY, set the temperature to 400°F, and set the time to 20 minutes. Select START/STOP to begin.

6. After 5 minutes, remove the basket and shake the wings. Reinsert the basket to resume cooking. Remove and shake the basket every 5 minutes until the chicken is fully cooked.

7. When the cooking is complete, remove the cooked chicken from the basket; cover to keep warm.

(continued)

Fried Chicken and Waffles *continued*

8. Rinse the basket and crisper plate with warm water. Insert them back into the unit.

9. Select AIR FRY, set the temperature to 360ºF, and set the time to 3 minutes. Select START/STOP to begin.

10. Once the unit is preheated, spray the crisper plate with cooking spray. Working in batches, place the frozen waffles into the basket. Do not stack them. Spray the waffles with cooking oil.

11. Select AIR FRY, set the temperature to 360ºF, and set the time to 6 minutes. Select START/STOP to begin.

12. When the cooking is complete, repeat steps 10 and 11 with the remaining waffles.

13. Serve the waffles with the chicken and a touch of maple syrup, if desired.

Per Serving: *Calories: 461; Total fat: 22g; Saturated fat: 5g; Cholesterol: 95mg; Sodium: 567mg; Carbohydrates: 45g; Fiber: 2g; Protein: 28g*

SUBSTITUTION TIP: You can substitute 4 to 6 chicken tenders for the chicken wings in this recipe. Dip the tenders in 1 egg beaten with 1 tablespoon water, then dip the tenders in a combination of ½ cup bread crumbs seasoned with garlic powder and chicken seasoning; press the crumbs so they stay attached. Air fry the tenders at 390°F for 10 to 15 minutes, turning once, until the chicken reaches 165°F.

Puffed Egg Tarts

PREP TIME: 10 MINUTES / COOK TIME: 17 TO 20 MINUTES / MAKES 2 TARTS / 390°F / BAKE

Puffed Egg Tarts are "fried" eggs baked on top of flaky, golden puff pastry. These tarts are layered with cheese, giving them an abundance of flavor. Served with a bowl of fruit, they make an elegant brunch. To change up the flavors, add a couple of asparagus spears or a handful of fresh spinach to this recipe.

⅓ **sheet frozen puff pastry, thawed**

Cooking oil spray

½ **cup shredded Cheddar cheese**

2 eggs

¼ **teaspoon salt, divided**

1 teaspoon minced fresh parsley (optional)

FAST, NUT FREE, VEGETARIAN

INGREDIENT TIP: Use caution when adding the eggs to the hot air fryer. Try placing each egg in a small bowl beforehand so you can pour it onto the tart. Also, puff pastry comes in a variety of sizes. Typically, the box will contain two sheets that are folded into thirds. Use one of the thirds for this recipe and cut that rectangle in half to form the two squares needed.

1. Insert the crisper plate into the basket and the basket into the unit. Preheat the unit by selecting BAKE, setting the temperature to 390°F, and setting the time to 3 minutes. Select START/STOP to begin.

2. Lay the puff pastry sheet on a piece of parchment paper and cut it in half.

3. Once the unit is preheated, spray the crisper plate with cooking oil. Transfer the 2 squares of pastry to the basket, keeping them on the parchment paper.

4. Select BAKE, set the temperature to 390°F, and set the time to 20 minutes. Select START/STOP to begin.

5. After 10 minutes, use a metal spoon to press down the center of each pastry square to make a well. Divide the cheese equally between the baked pastries. Carefully crack an egg on top of the cheese, and sprinkle each with the salt. Resume cooking for 7 to 10 minutes.

6. When the cooking is complete, the eggs will be cooked through. Sprinkle each with parsley (if using) and serve.

Per Serving *(1 tart): Calories: 322; Total fat: 24g; Saturated fat: 10g; Cholesterol: 216mg; Sodium: 598mg; Carbohydrates: 12g; Fiber: 0g; Protein: 15g*

Early Morning Steak and Eggs

PREP TIME: 8 MINUTES / COOK TIME: 14 MINUTES PER BATCH / SERVES 4 / 360°F, THEN 330°F
AIR FRY; BAKE

There's nothing quite like starting your day with hearty steak and eggs. And you won't believe just how fast the dish can be prepared in an air fryer. Note that you will need ramekins or heatproof custard cups for this recipe. Although this is a breakfast classic, you can use the same technique to cook this steak for a filling dinner, paired with baked potatoes or roasted vegetables.

Cooking oil spray

4 (4-ounce) New York strip steaks

1 teaspoon granulated garlic, divided

1 teaspoon salt, divided

1 teaspoon freshly ground black pepper, divided

Olive oil spray

4 eggs

½ teaspoon paprika

FAST, GLUTEN FREE

1. Insert the crisper plate into the basket and the basket into the unit. Preheat the unit by selecting AIR FRY, setting the temperature to 360°F, and setting the time to 3 minutes. Select START/STOP to begin.

2. Once the unit is preheated, spray the crisper plate with cooking oil. Place 2 steaks into the basket; do not oil or season them at this time.

3. Select AIR FRY, set the temperature to 360°F, and set the time to 9 minutes. Select START/STOP to begin.

4. After 5 minutes, open the unit and flip the steaks. Sprinkle each with ¼ teaspoon of granulated garlic, ¼ teaspoon of salt, and ¼ teaspoon of pepper. Resume cooking until the steaks register at least 145°F on a food thermometer.

5. When the cooking is complete, transfer the steaks to a plate and tent with aluminum foil to keep warm. Repeat steps 2, 3, and 4 with the remaining steaks.

6. Spray 4 ramekins with olive oil. Crack 1 egg into each ramekin. Sprinkle the eggs with the paprika and remaining ½ teaspoon each of salt and pepper. Working in batches, place 2 ramekins into the basket.

7. Select BAKE, set the temperature to 330°F, and set the time to 5 minutes. Select START/STOP to begin.

8. When the cooking is complete and the eggs are cooked to 160°F, remove the ramekins and repeat step 7 with the remaining 2 ramekins.

9. Serve the eggs with the steaks.

Per Serving *(1 steak and 1 egg): Calories: 304; Total fat: 19g; Saturated fat: 7g; Cholesterol: 261mg; Sodium: 653mg; Carbohydrates: 2g; Fiber: 0g; Protein: 31g*

AIR FRYER TIP: If you choose to make the eggs first, you will need to preheat your air fryer for about 5 minutes. But if you cook them second, the fryer will already be warm enough to get those eggs going right away. The eggs should be cooked last because they will cool much faster than the steak.

Air-Fried Spring
Rolls, page 48

4

Snacks and Appetizers

Air-Fried Spring Rolls

PREP TIME: 10 MINUTES / COOK TIME: 9 MINUTES / MAKES 16 SPRING ROLLS / 390°F / AIR FRY

These delicious spring rolls satisfy a craving for a fun snack, while being nutritious at the same time. Rice paper is gluten-free, healthy, and light—both in terms of fat content and texture. In the air fryer, these spring rolls come out just perfect: a little chewy and a little crispy.

4 teaspoons toasted sesame oil

6 medium garlic cloves, minced or pressed

1 tablespoon grated peeled fresh ginger

2 cups thinly sliced shiitake mushrooms

4 cups chopped green cabbage

1 cup grated carrot

½ teaspoon sea salt

16 rice paper wrappers

Cooking oil spray (sunflower, safflower, or refined coconut)

Gluten-free sweet and sour sauce or Thai sweet chili sauce, for serving (optional)

DAIRY FREE,
FAMILY FAVORITE,
FAST, GLUTEN FREE,
NUT FREE, VEGAN

1. Place a wok or sauté pan over medium heat until hot.

2. Add the sesame oil, garlic, ginger, mushrooms, cabbage, carrot, and salt. Cook for 3 to 4 minutes, stirring often, until the cabbage is lightly wilted. Remove the pan from the heat.

3. Gently run a rice paper under water. Lay it on a flat nonabsorbent surface (such as a countertop). Place about ¼ cup of the cabbage filling in the middle. Once the wrapper is soft enough to roll, fold the bottom up over the filling, fold in the sides, and roll the wrapper all the way up. (Basically, make a tiny burrito.)

4. Repeat step 3 to make the remaining spring rolls until you have the number of spring rolls you want to cook right now (and the amount that will fit in the air fryer basket in a single layer without them touching each other). Refrigerate any leftover filling in an airtight container for about 1 week.

5. Insert the crisper plate into the basket and the basket into the unit. Preheat the unit by selecting AIR FRY, setting the temperature to 390ºF, and setting the time to 3 minutes. Select START/STOP to begin.

6. Once the unit is preheated, spray the crisper plate and the basket with cooking oil. Place the spring rolls into the basket, leaving a little room between them so they don't stick to each other. Spray the top of each spring roll with cooking oil.

7. Select AIR FRY, set the temperature to 390ºF, and set the time to 9 minutes. Select START/STOP to begin.

8. When the cooking is complete, the egg rolls should be crisp-ish and lightly browned. Serve immediately, plain or with a sauce of choice.

Per Serving: *Calories: 65; Total fat: 2g; Saturated fat: 0g; Cholesterol: 0mg; Sodium: 112mg; Carbohydrates: 9g; Fiber: 1g; Protein: 1g*

SUBSTITUTION TIP: You can substitute wheat egg roll wrappers or even phyllo for the rice paper wrappers in this recipe, but it will no longer be gluten free. If you choose to use phyllo dough, layer three sheets together with a bit of butter before you fill and roll. Brush the edges of any of these alternative wrappers with a mixture of 1 egg yolk beaten with 1 tablespoon water so they stay together while they air fry.

INGREDIENT TIP: Not all rice paper wrappers are gluten free; some contain wheat flour. Be sure to read the label before you buy to make sure there's no wheat in the rice paper wrappers.

Classic French Fries

PREP TIME: 35 MINUTES / COOK TIME: 30 MINUTES / SERVES 6 / 390°F / AIR FRY

Few things compare to the mouthwatering goodness of hot, fresh French fries. These classic fries are ideal for weeknight dinners when you want to avoid fast food, but still crave those fries. So ditch the drive-through and make these at home for the family—with the air fryer, making perfect fries is easier than you think.

3 large russet potatoes, peeled and cut lengthwise into fry shapes

1 tablespoon canola oil

1 tablespoon extra-virgin olive oil

Salt

Freshly ground black pepper

Cooking oil spray

Fresh parsley, for garnish (optional)

DAIRY FREE, FAMILY FAVORITE, GLUTEN FREE, NUT FREE, VEGAN

1. Place the potatoes in a large bowl of cold water and let soak for at least 30 minutes, preferably 1 hour (see Ingredient Tip). Drain the potatoes and thoroughly dry them using a clean kitchen towel.

2. Insert the crisper plate into the basket and the basket into the unit. Preheat the unit by selecting AIR FRY, setting the temperature to 390°F, and setting the time to 3 minutes. Select START/STOP to begin.

3. Spread the fries onto a baking sheet (optional: lined with parchment paper) and coat them with the canola oil and olive oil. Season with salt and pepper.

4. Once the unit is preheated, spray the crisper plate with cooking oil. Place half the fries into the basket.

5. Select AIR FRY, set the temperature to 390°F, and set the time to 15 minutes. Select START/STOP to begin.

6. After 10 minutes, remove the basket and shake it so the fries at the bottom come up to the top. Reinsert the basket to resume cooking.

(continued)

Classic French Fries *continued*

7. When the cooking is complete, transfer the fries to a plate. Repeat steps 4, 5, 6, and 7 for the remaining fries.

8. When the second batch is complete, return all the fries to the basket and shake it. Air fry for 1 minute more so all the fries are hot before serving. Garnish with chopped parsley (if using).

Per Serving: *Calories: 168; Total fat: 5g; Saturated fat: 1g; Cholesterol: 0mg; Sodium: 38mg; Carbohydrates: 29g; Fiber: 4g; Protein: 3g*

INGREDIENT TIP: Soaking the potatoes in water removes excess starch from them. This results in crispy, crunchy fries. If you do not soak the potatoes first, they will likely turn out soft. You can prep and soak the potatoes up to 1 hour before air frying.

COOKING TIP: Use your judgment and overall preference to determine how long the fries should cook. If the fries need to be crispier, cook them longer. Really crisp fries may need to cook up to 20 minutes. Cooking time may also depend on how thick you cut your potatoes.

Apple Chips

PREP TIME: 5 MINUTES / COOK TIME: 7 TO 8 HOURS / SERVES 4 / 135°F / DEHYDRATE

Ditch your roll-ups and gummy snacks for this crunchy, healthy treat made from real fruit. Just use your air fryer to dehydrate apple slices for a crunchy, healthy treat. This recipe takes 7 to 8 hours, so set your air fryer and let it work while you sleep.

4 medium apples, any type, cored and cut into ½-inch-thick slices (thin slices yield crunchy chips)

¼ teaspoon ground cinnamon

¼ teaspoon ground nutmeg

FAMILY FAVORITE, FAST, GLUTEN FREE, NUT FREE, VEGAN

1. Place the apple slices in a large bowl. Sprinkle the cinnamon and nutmeg onto the apple slices and toss to coat.

2. Insert the crisper plate into the basket and the basket into the unit. Preheat the unit by selecting DEHYDRATE, setting the temperature to 135ºF, and setting the time to 3 minutes. Select START/STOP to begin.

3. Once the unit is preheated, place the apple chips into the basket. It is okay to stack them.

4. Select DEHYDRATE, set the temperature to 135ºF, and set the time to 7 or 8 hours. Select START/STOP to begin.

5. When the cooking is complete, cool the apple chips. Serve or store at room temperature in an airtight container for up to 1 week.

PREPARATION TIP: Thickly sliced apples will turn out mushy. Slice them as thinly as possible—using a mandoline helps. Don't spray the apples with cooking oil—if you do, the chips will taste burned. When the cooking is complete, let a chip cool for a bit, taste it, and use your judgment as to how much additional cooking time is needed.

AIR FRYER TIP: If you don't want to do the longer Dehydrate process, you can make these apple chips in mere minutes. Preheat the air fryer to 350°F and bake the apple slices for 10 minutes.

Per Serving: *Calories: 117; Total fat: 1g; Saturated fat: 0g; Cholesterol: 0mg; Sodium: 2mg; Carbohydrates: 31g; Fiber: 6g; Protein: 1g*

Easy Garlic-Parmesan French Fries

PREP TIME: 5 MINUTES / COOK TIME: 20 TO 25 MINUTES / SERVES 4 / 400°F / AIR FRY

French fries are a favorite snack to make in the air fryer. These fries are special because they are loaded with garlic and Parmesan cheese. Ready in about 25 minutes, they're perfect to serve with just about anything.

3 medium russet potatoes, rinsed, dried, and cut into thin wedges or classic fry shapes

2 tablespoons extra-virgin olive oil

1 tablespoon granulated garlic

⅓ cup grated Parmesan cheese

½ teaspoon salt

¼ teaspoon freshly ground black pepper

Cooking oil spray

2 tablespoons finely chopped fresh parsley (optional)

FAST, GLUTEN FREE,
NUT FREE, VEGETARIAN

1. In a large bowl combine the potato wedges or fries and the olive oil. Toss to coat.

2. Sprinkle the potatoes with the granulated garlic, Parmesan cheese, salt, and pepper, and toss again.

3. Insert the crisper plate into the basket and the basket into the unit. Preheat the unit by selecting AIR FRY, setting the temperature to 400°F, and setting the time to 3 minutes. Select START/STOP to begin.

4. Once the unit is preheated, spray the crisper plate with cooking oil. Place the potatoes into the basket.

5. Select AIR FRY, set the temperature to 400°F, and set the time to 20 to 25 minutes. Select START/STOP to begin.

(continued)

Easy Garlic-Parmesan French Fries *continued*

6. After about 10 minutes, remove the basket and shake it so the fries at the bottom come up to the top. Reinsert the basket to resume cooking.

7. When the cooking is complete, top the fries with the parsley (if using) and serve hot.

Per Serving: Calories: 180; Total fat: 10g; Saturated fat: 3g; Cholesterol: 6mg; Sodium: 444mg; Carbohydrates: 20g; Fiber: 2g; Protein: 6g

VARIATION TIP: Change up these already delicious fries by adding paprika, seasoning salt, or onion powder. You can also sprinkle them with some Cheddar cheese immediately after they are done for added deliciousness.

Onion Rings

PREP TIME: 15 MINUTES / COOK TIME: 14 MINUTES PER BATCH / SERVES 4 / 390°F / AIR FRY

These onion rings satisfy the need for a crunchy decadent snack, but are far healthier than the typical deep-fried variety. Don't overcrowd the onion rings in the air fryer; cook this recipe in two batches if necessary. Don't skimp on the cooking oil—it's important to achieve maximum delicious crunchiness. If you'd like to make onion rings for more people, simply multiply the recipe and cook in batches.

1 large white onion, peeled and cut into ½ to ¾-inch-thick slices (about 2 cups)

½ cup 2% milk

1 cup whole-wheat pastry flour, or all-purpose flour

2 tablespoons cornstarch

¾ teaspoon sea salt, divided

½ teaspoon freshly ground black pepper, divided

¾ teaspoon granulated garlic, divided

1½ cups whole-grain bread crumbs, or gluten-free bread crumbs (see Tip)

Cooking oil spray (coconut, sunflower, or safflower)

Ketchup, for serving (optional)

FAMILY FAVORITE, NUT FREE

1. Carefully separate the onion slices into rings—a gentle touch is important here.

2. Place the milk in a shallow bowl and set aside.

3. Make the first breading: In a medium bowl, stir together the flour, cornstarch, ¼ teaspoon of salt, ¼ teaspoon of pepper, and ¼ teaspoon of granulated garlic. Set aside.

4. Make the second breading: In a separate medium bowl, stir together the bread crumbs with the remaining ½ teaspoon of salt, the remaining ½ teaspoon of garlic, and the remaining ½ teaspoon of pepper. Set aside.

5. Insert the crisper plate into the basket and the basket into the unit. Preheat the unit by selecting AIR FRY, setting the temperature to 390ºF, and setting the time to 3 minutes. Select START/STOP to begin.

(continued)

Onion Rings *continued*

6. Once the unit is preheated, spray the crisper plate and the basket with cooking oil.

7. To make the onion rings, dip one ring into the milk and into the first breading mixture. Dip the ring into the milk again and back into the first breading mixture, coating thoroughly. Dip the ring into the milk one last time and then into the second breading mixture, coating thoroughly. Gently lay the onion ring in the basket. Repeat with additional rings and, as you place them into the basket, do not overlap them too much. Once all the onion rings are in the basket, generously spray the tops with cooking oil.

8. Select AIR FRY, set the temperature to 390ºF, and set the time to 14 minutes. Insert the basket into the unit. Select START/STOP to begin.

9. After 4 minutes, open the unit and spray the rings generously with cooking oil. Close the unit to resume cooking. After 3 minutes, remove the basket and spray the onion rings again. Remove the rings, turn them over, and place them back into the basket. Generously spray them again with oil. Reinsert the basket to resume cooking. After 4 minutes, generously spray the rings with oil one last time. Resume cooking for the remaining 3 minutes, or until the onion rings are very crunchy and brown.

10. When the cooking is complete, serve the hot rings with ketchup, or other sauce of choice.

COOKING TIP: It's easy to make bread crumbs yourself—and they're usually much healthier than store-bought varieties. Put a few slices of whole-grain bread in a food processor and pulse until finely crumbled. (You can also crumble the bread by hand.) Process several pieces of bread at once and freeze so they'll be ready to use when an onion ring emergency strikes.

Per Serving: Calories: 355; Total fat: 3g; Saturated fat: <1g; Cholesterol: 2mg; Sodium: 753mg; Carbohydrates: 73g; Fiber: 11g; Protein: 10g

Crunchy Pork Egg Rolls

PREP TIME: 15 MINUTES / COOK TIME: 12 MINUTES / MAKES 12 EGG ROLLS / 400°F / AIR FRY

Air-fried egg rolls far surpass the typical freebies Chinese restaurants throw in with your takeout order. These rolls are packed with tasty ground pork, fresh vegetables, and bold sauces, achieving mouthwatering flavor without the excessive grease. A basting brush can help you assemble your egg rolls.

Cooking oil spray

2 garlic cloves, minced

12 ounces ground pork

1 teaspoon sesame oil

¼ cup soy sauce

2 teaspoons grated peeled fresh ginger

2 cups shredded green cabbage

4 scallions, green parts (white parts optional), chopped

24 egg roll wrappers

DAIRY FREE, FAMILY FAVORITE, FAST, NUT FREE

1. Spray a skillet with the cooking oil and place it over medium-high heat. Add the garlic and cook for 1 minute until fragrant.

2. Add the ground pork to the skillet. Using a spoon, break the pork into smaller chunks.

3. In a small bowl, whisk the sesame oil, soy sauce, and ginger until combined. Add the sauce to the skillet. Stir to combine and continue cooking for about 5 minutes until the pork is browned and thoroughly cooked.

4. Stir in the cabbage and scallions. Transfer the pork mixture to a large bowl.

5. Lay the egg roll wrappers on a flat surface. Dip a basting brush in water and glaze each egg roll wrapper along the edges with the wet brush. This will soften the dough and make it easier to roll.

6. Stack 2 egg roll wrappers (it works best if you double-wrap the egg rolls). Scoop 1 to 2 tablespoons of the pork mixture into the center of each wrapper stack.

(continued)

Crunchy Pork Egg Rolls *continued*

7. Roll one long side of the wrappers up over the filling. Press firmly on the area with the filling, tucking it in lightly to secure it in place. Fold in the left and right sides. Continue rolling to close. Use the basting brush to wet the seam and seal the egg roll. Repeat with the remaining ingredients.

8. Insert the crisper plate into the basket and the basket into the unit. Preheat the unit by selecting AIR FRY, setting the temperature to 400ºF, and setting the time to 3 minutes. Select START/STOP to begin.

9. Once the unit is preheated, spray the crisper plate with cooking oil. Place the egg rolls into the basket. It is okay to stack them. Spray them with cooking oil.

10. Select AIR FRY, set the temperature to 400ºF, and set the time to 12 minutes. Insert the basket into the unit. Select START/STOP to begin.

11. After 8 minutes, use tongs to flip the egg rolls. Reinsert the basket to resume cooking.

12. When the cooking is complete, serve the egg rolls hot.

Per Serving: *Calories: 244; Total fat: 4g; Saturated fat: 1g; Cholesterol: 27mg; Sodium: 683mg; Carbohydrates: 39g; Fiber: 2g; Protein: 12g*

SUBSTITUTION TIP: Grated fresh ginger, or ginger sold in jars in the produce section of the grocery store, works best in this recipe, but you can use 1 teaspoon ground ginger, which can be found in the spice aisle.

COOKING TIP: When you open the air fryer at 8 minutes to flip the egg rolls, evaluate how much longer you think they need to cook. Touch them with a knife or fork to determine if they are crunchy enough.

Mushroom and Gruyère Tarts

These tarts may sound like a recipe for only the fanciest get-together, but they are incredibly easy to make in a pinch for impromptu guests—and they're sure to impress. They're creamy on the inside, with flaky, buttery layers on the outside, and you can bet that everyone will be fighting over the last one.

2 tablespoons extra-virgin olive oil, divided

1 small white onion, sliced

8 ounces shiitake mushrooms, sliced

¼ teaspoon sea salt

¼ teaspoon freshly ground black pepper

¼ cup dry white wine

1 sheet frozen puff pastry, thawed

1 cup shredded Gruyère cheese

Cooking oil spray

1 tablespoon thinly sliced fresh chives

NUT FREE, VEGETARIAN

1. Insert the crisper plate into the basket and the basket into the unit. Preheat the unit by selecting BAKE, setting the temperature to 300°F, and setting the time to 3 minutes. Select START/STOP to begin.

2. In a heatproof bowl that fits into the basket, stir together 1 tablespoon of olive oil, the onion, and the mushrooms.

3. Once the unit is preheated, place the bowl into the basket.

4. Select BAKE, set the temperature to 300°F, and set the time to 7 minutes. Select START/STOP to begin.

5. After about 2½ minutes, stir the vegetables. Resume cooking. After another 2½ minutes, the vegetables should be browned and tender. Season with the salt and pepper and add the wine. Resume cooking until the liquid evaporates, about 2 minutes.

6. When the cooking is complete, place the bowl on a heatproof surface.

(continued)

Mushroom and Gruyère Tarts *continued*

7. Increase the air fryer temperature to 390°F and set the time to 3 minutes. Select START/STOP to begin.

8. Unfold the puff pastry and cut it into 15 (3-by-3-inch) squares. Using a fork, pierce the dough and brush both sides with the remaining 1 tablespoon of olive oil.

9. Evenly distribute half the cheese among the puff pastry squares, leaving a ½-inch border around the edges. Divide the mushroom-onion mixture among the pastry squares and top with the remaining cheese.

10. Once the unit is preheated, spray the crisper plate with cooking oil. Working in batches, place 5 tarts into the basket; do not stack or overlap.

11. Select BAKE, set the temperature to 390°F, and set the time to 8 minutes. Select START/STOP to begin.

12. After 6 minutes, check the tarts; if not yet golden brown, resume cooking for about 2 minutes more.

13. When the cooking is complete, remove the tarts and transfer to a wire rack to cool. Repeat steps 10, 11, and 12 with the remaining tarts.

14. Serve garnished with the chives.

VARIATION TIP: You can change these tarts by varying the filling. Substitute cooked shredded chicken or cooked sausage or ground beef for the mushrooms. Use a different cheese, such as Monterey Jack, Muenster, or Havarti. Add some minced garlic or garnish the tarts with fresh thyme leaves instead of chives.

Per Serving *(3 tarts): Calories 214; Total fat: 14g; Saturated fat: 5g; Cholesterol: 20mg; Sodium: 190mg; Carbohydrates: 10g; Fiber: 1g; Protein: 8g*

Panko-Breaded Mozzarella Sticks

PREP TIME: 8 MINUTES / COOK TIME: 5 MINUTES / SERVES 4 / 400°F / AIR FRY

Fried mozzarella sticks are one of the best-loved appetizers in restaurants. Now, you can make them at home—thanks to your air fryer. These taste best eaten hot, and they won't stick around long! You can dip them in marinara sauce, but for the ultimate cheese experience, serve with a side of spicy queso.

½ cup all-purpose flour

1 egg, beaten

½ cup panko bread crumbs

½ cup grated
Parmesan cheese

1 teaspoon Italian seasoning

½ teaspoon garlic salt

6 mozzarella sticks, halved
crosswise

Olive oil spray

FAMILY FAVORITE, FAST,
NUT FREE, VEGETARIAN

1. Put the flour in a small bowl.

2. Put the beaten egg in another small bowl.

3. In a medium bowl, stir together the panko, Parmesan cheese, Italian seasoning, and garlic salt.

4. Roll a mozzarella-stick half in the flour, dip it into the egg, and then roll it in the panko mixture to coat. Press the coating lightly to make sure the bread crumbs stick to the cheese. Repeat with the remaining 11 mozzarella sticks.

5. Insert the crisper plate into the basket and the basket into the unit. Preheat the unit by selecting AIR FRY, setting the temperature to 400°F, and setting the time to 3 minutes. Select START/STOP to begin.

6. Once the unit is preheated, spray the crisper plate with olive oil and place a parchment paper liner in the basket. Place the mozzarella sticks into the basket and lightly spray them with olive oil.

7. Select AIR FRY, set the temperature to 400°F, and set the time to 5 minutes. Select START/STOP to begin.

8. When the cooking is complete, the mozzarella sticks should be golden and crispy. Let the sticks stand for 1 minute before transferring them to a serving plate. Serve warm.

Per Serving *(3 sticks): Calories: 297; Total fat: 14g; Saturated fat: 8g; Cholesterol: 81mg; Sodium: 575mg; Carbohydrates: 24g; Fiber: 1g; Protein: 20g*

AIR FRYER TIP: The air fryer will retain the heat for a while after you cook the first batch. If you are making additional batches, you may need to cook them for only 4 minutes instead of 5.

Scotch Eggs

PREP TIME: 15 MINUTES / COOK TIME: 11 TO 13 MINUTES / SERVES 6 / 375°F / AIR FRY

Scotch eggs are an English classic, made with a hardboiled egg encased in pork sausage and deep-fried. Here we lighten the recipe using chicken sausage and cooking it in the air fryer. These are great for a mid-morning or afternoon snack.

1½ pounds bulk lean chicken or turkey sausage

3 raw eggs, divided

1½ cups dried bread crumbs, divided

½ cup all-purpose flour

6 hardboiled eggs, peeled

Cooking oil spray

DAIRY FREE, FAMILY FAVORITE, FAST, NUT FREE

1. In a large bowl, combine the chicken sausage, 1 raw egg, and ½ cup of bread crumbs and mix well. Divide the mixture into 6 pieces and flatten each into a long oval.

2. In a shallow bowl, beat the remaining 2 raw eggs.

3. Place the flour in a small bowl.

4. Place the remaining 1 cup of bread crumbs in a second small bowl.

5. Roll each hardboiled egg in the flour and wrap one of the chicken sausage pieces around each egg to encircle it completely.

6. One at a time, roll the encased eggs in the flour, dip in the beaten eggs, and finally dip in the bread crumbs to coat.

7. Insert the crisper plate into the basket and the basket into the unit. Preheat the unit by selecting AIR FRY, setting the temperature to 375°F, and setting the time to 3 minutes. Select START/STOP to begin.

8. Once the unit is preheated, spray the crisper plate with cooking oil. Place the eggs in a single layer into the basket and spray them with oil.

(continued)

Scotch Eggs *continued*

9. Select AIR FRY, set the temperature to 375ºF, and set the time to 13 minutes. Select START/STOP to begin.

10. After about 6 minutes, use tongs to turn the eggs and spray them with more oil. Resume cooking for 5 to 7 minutes more, or until the chicken is thoroughly cooked and the Scotch eggs are browned.

11. When the cooking is complete, serve warm.

Per Serving: *Calories: 623; Total fat: 40g; Saturated fat: 13g; Cholesterol: 341mg; Sodium: 1,140mg; Carbohydrates: 28g; Fiber: 2g; Protein: 35g*

INGREDIENT TIP: You can buy hardboiled eggs, already peeled, at many grocery stores! Look for them in the dairy case, and make sure to follow expiration dates to the letter. Or hardboil them right in your air fryer. Just add whole eggs, in a single layer, to the air fryer basket. Bake at 270°F for 15 minutes. Remove the eggs from the fryer and put into ice water. Peel when they are cool.

Stuffed Jalapeño Poppers

PREP TIME: 12 MINUTES / COOK TIME: 6 TO 8 MINUTES / SERVES 10 / 375°F / AIR FRY

This classic appetizer is a cinch to make in the air fryer. Just mix the cream cheese with the seasonings, stuff the jalapeños, top with panko, and fry to crispy perfection. You can make these poppers vegan by using dairy-free cream cheese.

8 ounces cream cheese, at room temperature

1 cup panko bread crumbs, divided

2 tablespoons fresh parsley, minced

1 teaspoon chili powder

10 jalapeño peppers, halved and seeded

Cooking oil spray

FAST, NUT FREE, VEGETARIAN

VARIATION TIP: Change it up by sprinkling Cheddar cheese on top or mixing diced ham or cooked bacon bits into the cream cheese mixture. You could also use Havarti or Swiss cheese. Other good options include sprinkling the jalapeños with crushed potato chips or tortilla chips instead of the bread crumbs or adding chopped scallions to the cream cheese mixture.

1. In a small bowl, whisk the cream cheese, ½ cup of panko, the parsley, and chili powder until combined. Stuff the cheese mixture into the jalapeño halves.

2. Sprinkle the tops of the stuffed jalapeños with the remaining ½ cup of panko and press it lightly into the filling.

3. Insert the crisper plate into the basket and the basket into the unit. Preheat the unit by selecting AIR FRY, setting the temperature to 375°F, and setting the time to 3 minutes. Select START/STOP to begin.

4. Once the unit is preheated, spray the crisper plate with cooking oil. Place the poppers into the basket.

5. Select AIR FRY, set the temperature to 375°F, and set the time to 8 minutes. Select START/STOP to begin.

6. After 6 minutes, check the poppers. If they are softened and the cheese is melted, they are done. If not, resume cooking.

7. When the cooking is complete, serve warm.

Per Serving *(5 poppers): Calories: 636; Total fat: 43g; Saturated fat: 26g; Cholesterol: 125mg; Sodium: 747mg; Carbohydrates: 47g; Fiber: 5g; Protein: 17g*

Roasted Shishito Peppers
with Lime, page 72

5

Vegetables and Sides

Roasted Shishito Peppers with Lime

PREP TIME: 4 MINUTES / COOK TIME: 9 MINUTES / SERVES 4 / 390°F / AIR ROAST

Shishito peppers are a long skinny pepper with a heat scale somewhere between bell peppers and Anaheim peppers. Anaheim peppers and bell peppers are a great substitution if you can't find shishito peppers. They make a tasty snack or side dish when cooked in the air fryer.

Cooking oil spray (sunflower, safflower, or refined coconut)

1 pound shishito, Anaheim, or bell peppers, rinsed

1 tablespoon soy sauce

2 teaspoons freshly squeezed lime juice

2 large garlic cloves, pressed

DAIRY FREE, FAST, NUT FREE

1. Insert the crisper plate into the basket and the basket into the unit. Preheat the unit by selecting AIR ROAST, setting the temperature to 390°F, and setting the time to 3 minutes. Select START/STOP to begin.

2. Once the unit is preheated, spray the crisper plate and the basket with cooking oil. Place the peppers into the basket and spray them with oil.

3. Select AIR ROAST, set the temperature to 390°F, and set the time to 9 minutes. Select START/STOP to begin.

4. After 3 minutes, remove the basket and shake the peppers. Spray the peppers with more oil. Reinsert the basket to resume cooking. Repeat this step again after 3 minutes.

5. While the peppers roast, in a medium bowl, whisk the soy sauce, lime juice, and garlic until combined. Set aside.

6. When the cooking is complete, several of the peppers should have lots of nice browned spots on them. If using Anaheim or bell peppers, cut a slit in the side of each pepper and remove the seeds, which can be bitter.

7. Place the roasted peppers in the bowl with the sauce. Toss to coat the peppers evenly and serve.

Per Serving: Calories: 46; Total fat: 0g; Saturated fat: 0g; Cholesterol: 0mg; Sodium: 226mg; Carbohydrates: 9g; Fiber: 4g; Protein: 2g

INGREDIENT TIP: Shishito peppers can be found at farmers' markets, as well as most grocery stores. Tradition has it that one in every ten peppers is spicy, and the rest are mild.

Breaded Artichoke Hearts

PREP TIME: 15 MINUTES / COOK TIME: 8 MINUTES / SERVES 4 / 375°F / AIR FRY

Canned artichoke hearts are available at most grocery stores. Sometimes you can even find artichoke hearts in the freezer section. These warm and flaky panko-breaded artichoke hearts are designed to impress at dinner dates, parties, or events. No panko? Swap in regular bread crumbs for an equally delicious dish.

12 whole artichoke hearts packed in water, drained

½ cup all-purpose flour

1 egg

⅓ cup panko bread crumbs

1 teaspoon Italian seasoning

Cooking oil spray

DAIRY FREE, FAST, NUT FREE, VEGETARIAN

1. Squeeze any excess water from the artichoke hearts and place them on paper towels to dry.

2. Place the flour in a small bowl.

3. In another small bowl, beat the egg.

4. In a third small bowl, stir together the panko and Italian seasoning.

5. Dip the artichoke hearts in the flour, in the egg, and into the panko mixture until coated.

6. Insert the crisper plate into the basket and the basket into the unit. Preheat the unit by selecting AIR FRY, setting the temperature to 375°F, and setting the time to 3 minutes. Select START/STOP to begin.

7. Once the unit is preheated, spray the crisper plate and the basket with cooking oil. Place the breaded artichoke hearts into the basket, stacking them if needed.

8. Select AIR FRY, set the temperature to 375°F, and set the time to 8 minutes. Select START/STOP to begin.

9. After 4 minutes, use tongs to flip the artichoke hearts. I recommend flipping instead of shaking because the hearts are small, and this will help keep the breading intact. Re-insert the basket to resume cooking.

10. When the cooking is complete, the artichoke hearts should be deep golden brown and crisp. Cool for 5 minutes before serving.

Per Serving: *Calories: 134; Total fat: 1g; Saturated fat: <1g; Cholesterol: 46mg; Sodium: 407mg; Carbohydrates: 24g; Fiber: 3g; Protein: 6g*

INGREDIENT TIP: You can create your own Italian seasoning by combining ¼ teaspoon each of dried thyme, oregano, basil, and red pepper flakes.

COOKING TIP: Check on the artichokes throughout the cooking process to monitor doneness and adjust cook time as necessary.

Crispy Broccoli

PREP TIME: 10 MINUTES / COOK TIME: 9 TO 14 MINUTES PER BATCH / SERVES 4 / 390°F / AIR ROAST

When broccoli is roasted it becomes sweet and slightly crisp around the edges. This super-easy and healthy recipe will make broccoli lovers out of everyone! This makes an excellent side dish, or you can even serve it as an appetizer with a dip made from yogurt and salsa.

1 large head broccoli, rinsed and patted dry

2 teaspoons extra-virgin olive oil

1 tablespoon freshly squeezed lemon juice

Olive oil spray

FAMILY FAVORITE, GLUTEN FREE, NUT FREE, VEGAN

1. Cut off the broccoli florets and separate them. You can use the stems, too; peel the stems and cut them into 1-inch chunks.

2. Insert the crisper plate into the basket and the basket into the unit. Preheat the unit by selecting AIR ROAST, setting the temperature to 390ºF, and setting the time to 3 minutes. Select START/STOP to begin.

3. In a large bowl, toss together the broccoli, olive oil, and lemon juice until coated.

4. Once the unit is preheated, spray the crisper plate with olive oil. Working in batches, place half the broccoli into the basket.

5. Select AIR ROAST, set the temperature to 390ºF, and set the time to 14 minutes. Select START/STOP to begin.

(continued)

Crispy Broccoli *continued*

6. After 5 minutes, remove the basket and shake the broccoli. Reinsert the basket to resume cooking. Check the broccoli after 5 minutes. If it is crisp-tender and slightly brown around the edges, it is done. If not, resume cooking.

7. When the cooking is complete, transfer the broccoli to a serving bowl. Repeat steps 5 and 6 with the remaining broccoli. Serve immediately.

Per Serving: *Calories: 63; Fat: 2g; Saturated fat: 0g; Protein: 4g; Carbohydrates: 10g; Sodium: 50mg; Fiber: 4g; Sugar: 3g*

INGREDIENT TIP: You can cook cauliflower using this method, too! Just rinse it, cut it into florets, toss with the olive oil and lemon juice, and roast. It's delicious as a side dish or an appetizer.

Buffalo Cauliflower

PREP TIME: 15 MINUTES / COOK TIME: 5 TO 7 MINUTES PER BATCH / SERVES 6 / 375°F / AIR FRY

Everyone knows about Buffalo chicken wings—that deep-fried appetizer served with blue cheese sauce and loaded with fat and sodium. This side dish version is made with cauliflower instead of chicken wings, and the sauce is made with Greek yogurt, hot sauce, and just a bit of blue cheese.

1 large head cauliflower, rinsed and separated into small florets

1 tablespoon extra-virgin olive oil

½ teaspoon garlic powder

Cooking oil spray

⅓ cup hot wing sauce

⅔ cup nonfat Greek yogurt

¼ cup buttermilk

½ teaspoon hot sauce (such as Frank's RedHot or Tabasco)

1 celery stalk, chopped

2 tablespoons crumbled blue cheese

FAMILY FAVORITE, FAST, GLUTEN FREE, NUT FREE, VEGETARIAN

1. Insert the crisper plate into the basket and the basket into the unit. Preheat the unit by selecting AIR FRY, setting the temperature to 375°F, and setting the time to 3 minutes. Select START/STOP to begin.

2. In a large bowl, toss together the cauliflower florets and olive oil. Sprinkle with the garlic powder and toss again to coat.

3. Once the unit is preheated, spray the crisper plate with cooking oil. Put half the cauliflower into the basket.

4. Select AIR FRY, set the temperature to 375°F, and set the time to 7 minutes. Select START/STOP to begin.

5. After 3 minutes, remove the basket and shake the cauliflower. Reinsert the basket to resume cooking. After 2 minutes, check the cauliflower. It is done when it is browned. If not, resume cooking.

(continued)

Buffalo Cauliflower *continued*

6. When the cooking is complete, transfer the cauliflower to a serving bowl and toss with half the hot wing sauce.

7. Repeat steps 4, 5, and 6 with the remaining cauliflower and hot wing sauce.

8. In a small bowl, stir together the yogurt, buttermilk, hot sauce, celery, and blue cheese. Drizzle the sauce over the finished cauliflower and serve.

Per Serving: *Calories: 86; Fat: 3g; Saturated fat: 1g; Protein: 5g; Carbohydrates: 12g; Sodium: 79mg; Fiber: 4g; Sugar: 6g*

INGREDIENT TIP: Cauliflower is one of the most nutritious vegetables. It is a member of the cruciferous family, which means it contains compounds that may help reduce your risk of developing cancer and other diseases.

Nacho Kale Chips

PREP TIME: 7 MINUTES / COOK TIME: 5 MINUTES / MAKES ABOUT 40 CHIPS / 375°F / BAKE

Crunchy kale chips just got an upgrade. To give a little extra kick to your healthy snack, these chips are smothered in homemade nacho seasoning that makes them almost addictive. Not looking for the added spice? Make them with just kale, olive oil, and salt.

1 tablespoon chili powder

1 tablespoon nacho cheese powder

1 teaspoon ground cumin

½ teaspoon dried oregano

½ teaspoon garlic powder

¼ teaspoon onion powder

⅛ teaspoon paprika

4 cups loosely packed kale, stemmed and chopped into chip-size pieces

2 tablespoons extra-virgin olive oil

Cooking oil spray

FAST, GLUTEN FREE, NUT FREE, VEGETARIAN

VARIATION TIP: You can change these up by using prepackaged ranch seasoning instead of the homemade nacho seasoning. To make this recipe even faster, replace the homemade nacho seasoning mix with a packet of taco seasoning. You can find nacho cheese powder in the seasoning section of your local grocer.

1. In a small bowl, stir together the chili powder, nacho cheese powder, cumin, oregano, garlic powder, onion powder, and paprika.

2. In a medium bowl, drizzle the kale with olive oil and toss to coat. Sprinkle in the seasoning mix and toss again.

3. Insert the crisper plate into the basket and the basket into the unit. Preheat the unit by selecting BAKE, setting the temperature to 375°F, and setting the time to 3 minutes. Select START/STOP to begin.

4. Once the unit is preheated, spray the crisper plate with cooking oil. Transfer the kale to the basket.

5. Select BAKE, set the temperature to 375°F, and set the time to 5 minutes. Select START/STOP to begin.

6. After 2 minutes, remove the basket and shake the kale. Reinsert the basket to continue cooking.

7. When the cooking is complete, the chips should be dry and crisp.

Per Serving *(10 chips): Calories: 103; Total fat: 8g; Saturated fat: 1g; Cholesterol: 0mg; Sodium: 49mg; Carbohydrates: 9g; Fiber: 2g; Protein: 2g*

Fried Brussels Sprouts
with Honey-Sriracha Sauce

PREP TIME: 10 MINUTES / COOK TIME: 18 MINUTES / SERVES 4 / 390°F / AIR FRY

Crispy fried Brussels sprouts are a delicious twist on the classic roasted recipe. They are quick to prepare and cook. This healthy side dish works equally well for weeknight dinners or holiday meals. It combines bitter, spicy, and sweet flavors all in one.

1 teaspoon plus 1 tablespoon extra-virgin olive oil, divided

2 teaspoons minced garlic

2 tablespoons honey

1 tablespoon sugar

2 tablespoons freshly squeezed lemon juice

2 tablespoons rice vinegar

2 tablespoons sriracha

1 pound Brussels sprouts, stems trimmed and any tough leaves removed, rinsed, halved lengthwise, and dried

½ teaspoon salt

Cooking oil spray

DAIRY FREE, FAST, GLUTEN FREE, NUT FREE, VEGETARIAN

1. In a small saucepan over low heat, combine 1 teaspoon of olive oil, the garlic, honey, sugar, lemon juice, vinegar, and sriracha. Cook for 2 to 3 minutes, or until slightly thickened. Remove the pan from the heat, cover, and set aside.

2. Place the Brussels sprouts in a resealable bag or small bowl. Add the remaining olive oil and the salt, and toss to coat.

3. Insert the crisper plate into the basket and the basket into the unit. Preheat the unit by selecting AIR FRY, setting the temperature to 390°F, and setting the time to 3 minutes. Select START/STOP to begin.

4. Once the unit is preheated, spray the crisper plate with cooking oil. Add the Brussels sprouts to the basket.

5. Select AIR FRY, set the temperature to 390°F, and set the time to 15 minutes. Select START/STOP to begin.

(continued)

Fried Brussels Sprouts with Honey-Sriracha Sauce *continued*

6. After 7 or 8 minutes, remove the basket and shake it to toss the sprouts. Reinsert the basket to resume cooking.

7. When the cooking is complete, the leaves should be crispy and light brown and the sprout centers tender.

8. Place the sprouts in a medium serving bowl and drizzle the sauce over the top. Toss to coat, and serve immediately.

Per Serving: Calories: 144; Total fat: 5g; Saturated fat: 1g; Cholesterol: 0mg; Sodium: 411mg; Carbohydrates: 24g; Fiber: 4g; Protein: 4g

VARIATION TIP: Try sprinkling the Brussels sprouts with a little Parmesan cheese when serving for a savory surprise. Omit the sriracha if you don't like really spicy food; instead, substitute plain hot sauce or use seafood cocktail sauce.

Savory Roasted Sweet Potatoes

PREP TIME: 10 MINUTES / COOK TIME: 25 MINUTES / SERVES 4 / 330°F / AIR ROAST

Sweet potatoes are delicious when cooked with brown sugar and topped with marshmallows in the classic holiday casserole. But have you ever made them with savory ingredients? This easy recipe is especially tasty served alongside meatloaf or a pot roast.

Cooking oil spray

2 sweet potatoes, peeled and cut into 1-inch cubes

1 tablespoon extra-virgin olive oil

Pinch salt

Freshly ground black pepper

½ teaspoon dried thyme

½ teaspoon dried marjoram

¼ cup grated Parmesan cheese

FAMILY FAVORITE, GLUTEN FREE, NUT FREE, VEGETARIAN

INGREDIENT TIP: Raw sweet potatoes are very hard and difficult to cut into pieces. Use a sharp knife and take your time. First slice the potatoes lengthwise, then lengthwise again. Cut each stick into cubes. Sweet potatoes are high in vitamin A and are usually bright orange in color.

1. Insert the crisper plate into the basket and the basket into the unit. Preheat the unit by selecting AIR ROAST, setting the temperature to 330°F, and setting the time to 3 minutes. Select START/STOP to begin.

2. Once the unit is preheated, spray the crisper plate with cooking oil. Put the sweet potato cubes into the basket and drizzle with olive oil. Toss gently to coat. Sprinkle with the salt, pepper, thyme, and marjoram and toss again.

3. Select AIR ROAST, set the temperature to 330°F, and set the time to 25 minutes. Select START/STOP to begin.

4. After 10 minutes, remove the basket and shake the potatoes. Reinsert the basket to resume cooking. After another 10 minutes, remove the basket and shake the potatoes one more time. Sprinkle evenly with the Parmesan cheese. Reinsert the basket to resume cooking.

5. When the cooking is complete, the potatoes should be tender. Serve immediately.

Per Serving: *Calories: 186; Total fat: 5g; Saturated fat: 2g; Cholesterol: 5mg; Sodium: 115mg; Carbohydrates: 32g; Fiber: 5g; Protein: 4g*

Roasted Corn on the Cob

When roasted in the air fryer, this corn on the cob tastes like it was grilled outdoors. And it's ready in minutes; there's no need to wait for the grill to get to temperature. Serve alongside your barbecue favorites.

4 ears corn, shucked and halved crosswise

1 tablespoon extra-virgin olive oil

Salt

Freshly ground black pepper

Cooking oil spray

FAMILY FAVORITE, FAST, GLUTEN FREE, NUT FREE, VEGAN

SUBSTITUTION TIP: Use 1 tablespoon melted butter instead of the olive oil (but the recipe will no longer be vegan). Or, slather the hot roasted corn with butter before serving.

1. Insert the crisper plate into the basket and the basket into the unit. Preheat the unit by selecting AIR ROAST, setting the temperature to 390°F, and setting the time to 3 minutes. Select START/STOP to begin.

2. Place the corn in a large bowl. Coat with the olive oil and season with salt and pepper to taste.

3. Once the unit is preheated, spray the crisper plate with cooking oil. Place the corn into the basket.

4. Select AIR ROAST, set the temperature to 390°F, and set the time to 6 minutes. Select START/STOP to begin.

5. When the cooking is complete, let the corn cool for 5 minutes before serving.

Per Serving: *Calories: 93; Total fat: 4g; Saturated fat: 1g; Cholesterol: 0mg; Sodium: 50mg; Carbohydrates: 14g; Fiber: 2g; Protein: 2g*

Glazed Carrots and Sweet Potatoes

PREP TIME: 5 MINUTES / COOK TIME: 20 TO 25 MINUTES / SERVES 4 / 400°F / AIR ROAST

Carrots and sweet potatoes are two of the healthiest vegetables you can eat. They are packed with fiber and lots of vitamin A. This is an excellent recipe for the holidays. The air fryer will free up your oven and stovetop for other recipes. The honey-orange glaze on these root vegetables is delicious and easy to make.

2 large carrots, cut into 1-inch chunks

1 medium sweet potato, peeled and cut into 1-inch cubes

½ cup chopped onion

2 garlic cloves, minced

2 tablespoons honey

1 tablespoon freshly squeezed orange juice

2 teaspoons butter, melted

FAMILY FAVORITE, FAST, GLUTEN FREE, NUT FREE, VEGETARIAN

INGREDIENT TIP: The sweet potatoes you buy in the supermarket are not yams. Yams are drier and starchier, usually with a white-colored flesh that is not as sweet as sweet potatoes. Buy sweet potatoes that are firm with no soft spots.

1. Insert the crisper plate into the basket and the basket into the unit. Preheat the unit by selecting AIR ROAST, setting the temperature to 400°F, and setting the time to 3 minutes. Select START/STOP to begin.

2. In a 6-by-2-inch round pan, toss together the carrots, sweet potato, onion, garlic, honey, orange juice, and melted butter to coat.

3. Once the unit is preheated, place the pan into the basket.

4. Select AIR ROAST, set the temperature to 400°F, and set the time to 25 minutes. Select START/STOP to begin.

5. After 15 minutes, remove the basket and shake the vegetables. Reinsert the basket to resume cooking. After 5 minutes, if the vegetables are tender and glazed, they are done. If not, resume cooking.

6. When the cooking is complete, serve immediately.

Per Serving: *Calories: 105; Fat: 2g; Saturated fat: 1g; Protein: 1g; Carbohydrates: 21g; Sodium: 59mg; Fiber: 2g; Sugar: 13g*

Fried Green Tomatoes

PREP TIME: 15 MINUTES / COOK TIME: 30 MINUTES / SERVES 4 / 400°F / AIR FRY

Repopularized in the early 1990s by the movie of the same name, fried green tomatoes are a hallmark of Southern cuisine. In the air fryer, these battered unripe tomatoes transform into a mouthwatering treat—crispy on the outside and soft on the inside. Serve them as a side dish with your favorite main or as an appetizer with a side of ranch dip or aioli.

½ cup all-purpose flour

2 eggs

½ cup yellow cornmeal

½ cup panko bread crumbs

1 teaspoon garlic powder

Salt

Freshly ground black pepper

2 green tomatoes, cut into ½-inch-thick rounds

Cooking oil spray

DAIRY FREE, FAMILY FAVORITE, NUT FREE, VEGETARIAN

1. Place the flour in a small bowl.

2. In another small bowl, beat the eggs.

3. In a third small bowl, stir together the cornmeal, panko, and garlic powder. Season with salt and pepper.

4. Dip each tomato slice into the flour, the egg, and finally the cornmeal mixture to coat.

5. Insert the crisper plate into the basket and the basket into the unit. Preheat the unit by selecting AIR FRY, setting the temperature to 400ºF, and setting the time to 3 minutes. Select START/STOP to begin.

6. Once the unit is preheated, spray the crisper plate and the basket with cooking oil. Working in batches, place the tomato slices in the air fryer in a single layer. Do not stack them. Spray the tomato slices with the cooking oil.

7. Select AIR FRY, set the temperature to 400ºF, and set the time to 10 minutes. Select START/STOP to begin.

8. After 5 minutes, use tongs to flip the tomatoes. Resume cooking for 4 to 5 minutes, or until crisp.

9. When the cooking is complete, transfer the fried green tomatoes to a plate. Repeat steps 6, 7, and 8 for the remaining tomatoes.

Per Serving: Calories: 167; Total fat: 3g; Saturated fat: 1g; Cholesterol: 82mg; Sodium: 96mg; Carbohydrates: 28g; Fiber: 3g; Protein: 7g

SUBSTITUTION TIP: Standard bread crumbs can be used as a substitute for panko. Reduce the amount to ⅛ cup.

INGREDIENT TIP: You can find unripe green tomatoes at your local farmers' market in the spring, summer, and fall. There's really no substitute for this ingredient, so only make this recipe when you have unripe tomatoes.

Eggplant Parmesan

PREP TIME: 15 MINUTES / COOK TIME: 30 MINUTES / SERVES 4 / 400°F / AIR FRY

Here is a yummy option for Meatless Monday! Eggplant Parmesan is an Italian dish featuring eggplant slathered in marinara and melted cheese, served over pasta. When cooked in the air fryer, this classic stays crunchy on the outside and tender on the inside.

1 medium eggplant, peeled and cut into ½-inch-thick rounds

1 teaspoon salt, plus more for seasoning

½ cup all-purpose flour

2 eggs

¾ cup Italian bread crumbs

2 tablespoons grated Parmesan cheese

Freshly ground black pepper

Cooking oil spray

¾ cup marinara sauce

½ cup shredded Parmesan cheese, divided

½ cup shredded mozzarella cheese, divided

FAMILY FAVORITE,
NUT FREE, VEGETARIAN

1. Blot the eggplant with paper towels to dry completely. You can also sprinkle with 1 teaspoon of salt to sweat out the moisture; if you do this, rinse the eggplant slices and blot dry again.

2. Place the flour in a shallow bowl.

3. In another shallow bowl, beat the eggs.

4. In a third shallow bowl, stir together the bread crumbs and grated Parmesan cheese and season with salt and pepper.

5. Dip each eggplant round in the flour, in the eggs, and into the bread crumbs to coat.

6. Insert the crisper plate into the basket and the basket into the unit. Preheat the unit by selecting AIR FRY, setting the temperature to 400°F, and setting the time to 3 minutes. Select START/STOP to begin.

7. Once the unit is preheated, spray the crisper plate and the basket with cooking oil. Working in batches, place the eggplant rounds into the basket. Do not stack them. Spray the eggplant with the cooking oil.

8. Select AIR FRY, set the temperature to 400°F, and set the time to 10 minutes. Select START/STOP to begin.

9. After 7 minutes, open the unit and top each round with 1 teaspoon of marinara sauce and ½ tablespoon each of shredded Parmesan and mozzarella cheese. Resume cooking for 2 to 3 minutes until the cheese melts.

10. Repeat steps 5, 6, 7, 8, and 9 with the remaining eggplant.

11. When the cooking is complete, serve immediately.

INGREDIENT TIP: Fresh Parmesan cheese that you grate or shred yourself melts better than pre-grated and pre-shredded options. If you want to use fresh mozzarella, top each piece of eggplant with a thinly sliced round and monitor the cooking time closely to make sure the cheese fully melts.

Per Serving: *Calories: 310; Total fat: 9g; Saturated fat: 4g; Cholesterol: 97mg; Sodium: 844mg; Carbohydrates: 42g; Fiber: 7g; Protein: 16g*

Salmon on a Bed of
Fennel and Carrot, page 96

6

Fish and Seafood

Salmon on a Bed of Fennel and Carrot

PREP TIME: 15 MINUTES / COOK TIME: 15 MINUTES / SERVES 4 / 400°F / AIR ROAST

Salmon cooked on a bed of fennel and carrot is a fabulous dish for a special meal. Fennel has a light licorice-like flavor that is a great contrast to the sweet carrots and rich and smooth fish. And the sweet carrots add a touch of color to this recipe.

1 fennel bulb, thinly sliced

2 large carrots, sliced

1 large onion, thinly sliced

2 teaspoons extra-virgin olive oil

½ cup sour cream

1 teaspoon dried tarragon leaves

4 (5-ounce) salmon fillets

⅛ teaspoon salt

¼ teaspoon coarsely ground black pepper

FAST, GLUTEN FREE, NUT FREE

SUBSTITUTION TIP: You can use other fish fillets in this easy recipe, but remember that most fillets will cook more quickly than salmon. Orange roughy or halibut fillets will cook in about 5 to 7 minutes. Just use your food thermometer every time you cook meat, poultry, or fish to ensure correct cooking.

1. Insert the crisper plate into the basket and the basket into the unit. Preheat the unit by selecting AIR ROAST, setting the temperature to 400°F, and setting the time to 3 minutes. Select START/STOP to begin.

2. In a medium bowl, toss together the fennel, carrots, and onion. Add the olive oil and toss again to coat the vegetables. Put the vegetables into a 6-inch round metal pan.

3. Once the unit is preheated, place the pan into the basket.

4. Select AIR ROAST, set the temperature to 400°F, and set the time to 15 minutes. Select START/STOP to begin.

5. After 5 minutes, the vegetables should be crisp-tender. Remove the pan and stir in the sour cream and tarragon. Top with the salmon fillets and sprinkle the fish with the salt and pepper. Reinsert the pan into the basket and resume cooking.

6. When the cooking is complete, the salmon should flake easily with a fork and a food thermometer should register at least 145°F. Serve the salmon on top of the vegetables.

Per Serving: *Calories: 253; Fat 9g; Saturated fat: 1g; Protein: 31g; Carbohydrates: 12g; Sodium: 115mg; Fiber 3g; Sugar: 5g*

Louisiana Fried Catfish

PREP TIME: 10 MINUTES / COOK TIME: 20 MINUTES / SERVES 4 / 400°F / AIR FRY

Crispy golden-fried catfish coated in zesty Southern spices is a perennial favorite. This dish is traditionally battered in buttermilk and deep-fried. This air fryer version is lighter and healthier, yet every bit as good as Grandma used to make.

1 egg

⅔ cup finely ground cornmeal

¼ cup all-purpose flour

¾ teaspoon salt

1 teaspoon paprika

1 teaspoon Old Bay seasoning

¼ teaspoon garlic powder

¼ teaspoon freshly ground black pepper

4 (5-ounce) catfish fillets, halved crosswise

Olive oil spray

DAIRY FREE, FAST, NUT FREE

1. In a shallow bowl, beat the egg with 2 tablespoons water.

2. On a plate, stir together the cornmeal, flour, salt, paprika, Old Bay, garlic powder, and pepper.

3. Dip the fish into the egg mixture and into the cornmeal mixture to coat. Press the cornmeal mixture into the fish and gently shake off any excess.

4. Insert the crisper plate into the basket and the basket into the unit. Preheat the unit by selecting AIR FRY, setting the temperature to 400ºF, and setting the time to 3 minutes. Select START/STOP to begin.

5. Once the unit is preheated, place a parchment paper liner into the basket. Place the coated fish on the liner and spray it with olive oil.

6. Select AIR FRY, set the temperature to 400ºF, and set the time to 20 minutes. Select START/STOP to begin.

(continued)

Louisiana Fried Catfish *continued*

7. After 10 minutes, remove the basket and spray the fish with olive oil. Flip the fish and spray the other side with olive oil. Reinsert the basket to resume cooking. Check the fish after 7 minutes more. If the fish is golden and crispy and registers at least 145ºF on a food thermometer, it is ready. If not, resume cooking.

8. When the cooking is complete, serve.

INGREDIENT TIP: Adjust the cooking time depending on the thickness of your fillets. Try not to use ultra-thin fillets, as they tend to fall apart when flipping. Fish fillets should be at least ½-inch thick to cook properly in the air fryer.

Per Serving: Calories: 225; Total fat: 5g; Saturated fat: 1g; Cholesterol: 112mg; Sodium: 670mg; Carbohydrates: 22g; Fiber: 2g; Protein: 23g

Lemongrass Steamed Tuna

PREP TIME: 10 MINUTES / COOK TIME: 10 MINUTES / SERVES 4 / 390°F / BAKE

Steaming tuna produces very delicate results. The ingredients featured here are common in many styles of Southeast Asian cooking, and include lemongrass, soy sauce, sesame oil, rice wine vinegar, and fresh ginger. This combination of salt, acid, and piquant spices lends a complex flavor to this recipe, which comes together in just a few minutes.

4 small tuna steaks

2 tablespoons low-sodium soy sauce

2 teaspoons sesame oil

2 teaspoons rice wine vinegar

1 teaspoon grated peeled fresh ginger

⅛ teaspoon freshly ground black pepper

1 stalk lemongrass, bent in half

3 tablespoons freshly squeezed lemon juice

DAIRY FREE, FAMILY FAVORITE, FAST, NUT FREE

AIR FRYER TIP: Keep an eye on the liquid in the pan below the air fryer basket when this recipe is cooking. The tuna will give off liquid as it cooks and you don't want the pan to overflow.

1. Place the tuna steaks on a plate.

2. In a small bowl, whisk the soy sauce, sesame oil, vinegar, and ginger until combined. Pour this mixture over the tuna and gently rub it into both sides. Sprinkle the fish with the pepper. Let marinate for 10 minutes.

3. Insert the crisper plate into the basket and the basket into the unit. Preheat the unit by selecting BAKE, setting the temperature to 390°F, and setting the time to 3 minutes. Select START/STOP to begin.

4. Once the unit is preheated, place the lemongrass into the basket and top it with the tuna steaks. Drizzle the tuna with the lemon juice and 1 tablespoon of water.

5. Select BAKE, set the temperature to 390°F, and set the time to 10 minutes. Select START/STOP to begin.

6. When the cooking is complete, a food thermometer inserted into the tuna should register at least 145°F. Discard the lemongrass and serve the tuna.

Per Serving: Calories: 292; Total fat: 14g; Saturated fat: 3g; Cholesterol: 44mg; Sodium: 513mg; Carbohydrates: 1g; Fiber: 0g; Protein: 38g

Beer-Battered Fish and Chips

PREP TIME: 5 MINUTES / COOK TIME: 30 MINUTES / SERVES 4 / 400°F / AIR FRY

If you have never visited England and had their fish and chips, this is the closest you'll get! Beer in the batter adds wonderful flavor. Malty beer works best for this recipe, but substitute water or fish stock if you'd like.

1 cup all-purpose flour

½ cup cornstarch

1 teaspoon garlic powder

Salt

Freshly ground black pepper

2 eggs

1 cup malty beer

4 (4-ounce) cod fillets

Cooking oil spray

1 recipe Classic French Fries (page 51)

DAIRY FREE, FAMILY FAVORITE, NUT FREE

1. In a medium bowl, stir together the flour, cornstarch, and garlic powder, and season with salt and pepper.

2. In a medium bowl, beat the eggs with the beer.

3. Dip each cod fillet in the flour-cornstarch mixture and then in the egg-beer mixture. Dip the cod in the flour and cornstarch a second time.

4. Insert the crisper plate into the basket and the basket into the unit. Preheat the unit by selecting AIR FRY, setting the temperature to 400°F, and setting the time to 3 minutes. Select START/STOP to begin.

5. Once the unit is preheated, spray the crisper plate and the basket with cooking oil. Working in batches, place the cod into the basket; do not stack. Spray the fish with the cooking oil.

6. Select AIR FRY, set the temperature to 400°F, and set the time to 15 minutes. Select START/STOP to begin.

(continued)

Beer-Battered Fish and Chips *continued*

7. After 8 minutes, remove the basket, flip the fillets, and spray again with oil. Reinsert the basket to resume cooking. The fish is done when it flakes easily with a fork and temperature registers at least 145ºF on a food thermometer.

8. Repeat steps 5, 6, and 7 for the remaining fillets.

9. When the cooking is complete, serve with Classic French Fries (page 51).

Per Serving (fish and fries): Calories: 577; Total fat: 11g; Saturated fat: 2g; Cholesterol: 137mg; Sodium: 201mg; Carbohydrates: 84g; Fiber: 7g; Protein: 30g

INGREDIENT TIP: Malty beer has a sweet, nutty flavor, and not a lot of hops. Malt is made from barley, or other cereal grains such as wheat, rye, or oats, which is fermented or germinated.

Classic Fish Sandwiches with Quick Tartar Sauce

PREP TIME: 8 MINUTES / COOK TIME: 17 MINUTES / SERVES 4 / 400°F / AIR FRY

In this recipe, crispy, panko-coated tilapia is fried until golden brown and topped with homemade tartar sauce on a hoagie roll. This makes a great lunch, especially when served with a side of fresh carrots and celery or a bowl of coleslaw.

¾ cup mayonnaise

2 tablespoons dried minced onion

1 dill pickle spear, finely chopped

2 teaspoons pickle juice

¼ teaspoon salt

⅛ teaspoon freshly ground black pepper

⅓ cup all-purpose flour

1 egg, lightly beaten

1¾ cups panko bread crumbs

2 teaspoons lemon pepper

4 (6-ounce) tilapia fillets

Olive oil spray

4 hoagie rolls

4 butter lettuce leaves

DAIRY FREE, FAMILY FAVORITE, FAST, NUT FREE

1. To make the tartar sauce, in a small bowl, whisk the mayonnaise, dried onion, pickle, pickle juice, salt, and pepper until blended. Refrigerate while you make the fish.

2. Scoop the flour onto a plate; set aside.

3. Put the beaten egg in a medium shallow bowl.

4. On another plate, stir together the panko and lemon pepper.

5. Insert the crisper plate into the basket and the basket into the unit. Preheat the unit by selecting AIR FRY, setting the temperature to 400°F, and setting the time to 3 minutes. Select START/STOP to begin.

6. Dredge the tilapia fillets in the flour, in the egg, and press into the panko mixture to coat.

(continued)

Classic Fish Sandwiches with Quick Tartar Sauce *continued*

7. Once the unit is preheated, spray the crisper plate with olive oil and place a parchment paper liner into the basket. Place the prepared fillets on the liner in a single layer. Lightly spray the fillets with olive oil.

8. Select AIR FRY, set the temperature to 400ºF, and set the time to 17 minutes. Select START/STOP to begin.

9. After 8 minutes, remove the basket, carefully flip the fillets, and spray them with more olive oil. Reinsert the basket to resume cooking.

10. When the cooking is complete, the fillets should be golden and crispy and a food thermometer should register 145ºF. Place each cooked fillet in a hoagie roll, top with a little bit of tartar sauce and lettuce, and serve.

INGREDIENT TIP: You can use frozen tilapia for this recipe. Just thaw in the refrigerator for at least 8 hours before cooking.

Per Serving: *Calories: 779; Total fat: 35g; Saturated fat: 6g; Cholesterol: 133mg; Sodium: 1,153mg; Carbohydrates: 71g; Fiber: 5g; Protein: 48g*

Crunchy Baja Fish Tacos with Mango Salsa

PREP TIME: 15 MINUTES / COOK TIME: 17 MINUTES / SERVES 4 / 375°F / AIR FRY

Add surfside flair to your Taco Tuesday with these Baja-inspired tacos. They are coated in a beer wash and a spicy batter before being air fried to golden perfection. The zesty mango salsa adds sweetness and more heat. Optional toppings include shredded cabbage, julienned carrots, cheese, scallions, tomatoes, and avocado.

1 mango, peeled and diced

1 small jalapeño pepper, diced

½ red bell pepper, diced

½ red onion, minced

Pinch chopped fresh cilantro

Juice of ½ lime

¼ teaspoon salt

¼ teaspoon ground black pepper

½ cup Mexican beer (such as Corona or Dos Equis)

1 egg

¾ cup cornstarch

¾ cup all-purpose flour

½ teaspoon ground cumin

¼ teaspoon chili powder

1 pound cod, cut into 4 pieces

Olive oil spray

4 corn tortillas, or flour tortillas, at room temperature

DAIRY FREE, FAMILY FAVORITE, NUT FREE

1. In a small bowl, stir together the mango, jalapeño, red bell pepper, red onion, cilantro, lime juice, salt, and pepper. Set aside.

2. In a medium bowl, whisk the beer and egg.

3. In another medium bowl, stir together the cornstarch, flour, cumin, and chili powder.

4. Insert the crisper plate into the basket and the basket into the unit. Preheat the unit by selecting AIR FRY, setting the temperature to 375ºF, and setting the time to 3 minutes. Select START/STOP to begin.

5. Dip the fish pieces into the egg mixture and in the flour mixture to coat completely.

(continued)

Crunchy Baja Fish Tacos with Mango Salsa *continued*

6. Once the unit is preheated, place a parchment paper liner into the basket. Place the fish on the liner in a single layer.

7. Select AIR FRY, set the temperature to 375ºF, and set the time to 17 minutes. Select START/STOP to begin.

8. After about 9 minutes, spray the fish with olive oil. Reinsert the basket to resume cooking.

9. When the cooking is complete, the fish should be golden and crispy. Place the pieces in the tortillas, top with the mango salsa, and serve.

INGREDIENT TIP: Mexican beers are made with a yeast strain specifically from Mexico, giving the beer and the recipe a distinct flavor. However, this dish can be made with any golden lager available.

Per Serving: *Calories: 433; Total fat: 3g; Saturated fat: 1g; Cholesterol: 109mg; Sodium: 267mg; Carbohydrates: 61g; Fiber: 4g; Protein: 31g*

Cilantro-Lime Fried Shrimp

PREP TIME: 40 MINUTES / COOK TIME: 10 MINUTES / SERVES 4 / 400°F / AIR FRY

The zesty, bold flavors in this recipe celebrate spring and summer. Marinating the shrimp makes up most of the prep time. (You will need a resealable plastic bag for this step.) Feel free to use fresh or thawed frozen shrimp for this recipe. These shrimp are excellent dipped in purchased or homemade cocktail sauce.

1 pound raw large shrimp, peeled and deveined with tails on or off

½ cup chopped fresh cilantro

Juice of 1 lime

½ cup all-purpose flour

1 egg

¾ cup bread crumbs

Salt

Freshly ground black pepper

Cooking oil spray

1 cup cocktail sauce

DAIRY FREE, FAMILY FAVORITE, NUT FREE

1. Place the shrimp in a resealable plastic bag and add the cilantro and lime juice. Seal the bag. Shake it to combine. Marinate the shrimp in the refrigerator for 30 minutes.

2. Place the flour in a small bowl.

3. In another small bowl, beat the egg.

4. Place the bread crumbs in a third small bowl, season with salt and pepper, and stir to combine.

5. Insert the crisper plate into the basket and the basket into the unit. Preheat the unit by selecting AIR FRY, setting the temperature to 400°F, and setting the time to 3 minutes. Select START/STOP to begin.

6. Remove the shrimp from the plastic bag. Dip each in the flour, the egg, and the bread crumbs to coat. Gently press the crumbs onto the shrimp.

7. Once the unit is preheated, spray the crisper plate and the basket with cooking oil. Place the shrimp in the basket. It is okay to stack them. Spray the shrimp with the cooking oil.

(continued)

Cilantro-Lime Fried Shrimp *continued*

8. Select AIR FRY, set the temperature to 400ºF, and set the time to 8 minutes. Select START/STOP to begin.

9. After 4 minutes, remove the basket and flip the shrimp one at a time. Reinsert the basket to resume cooking.

10. When the cooking is complete, the shrimp should be crisp. Let cool for 5 minutes. Serve with cocktail sauce.

Per Serving: *Calories: 347; Total fat: 5g; Saturated fat: 1g; Cholesterol: 217mg; Sodium: 997mg; Carbohydrates: 42g; Fiber: 3g; Protein: 30g*

INGREDIENT TIP: Don't marinate the shrimp any longer than 30 minutes or they will be mushy. That rule holds true for any marinade that is acidic—made with lemon juice, lime juice, or grapefruit juice.

PREPARATION TIP: If using frozen shrimp, place the shrimp in a large bowl of cold water to thaw. Allow the shrimp to soak for 15 minutes. Drain and pat dry.

Island Coconut Shrimp with Pineapple Sauce

PREP TIME: 10 MINUTES / COOK TIME: 18 MINUTES / SERVES 4 / 400°F / AIR FRY

You can't go wrong with this dish, which features shrimp coated in coconut and air fried until golden brown. Served with an irresistible sweet and tangy pineapple sauce, this dish will make you feel like you are in a surfside restaurant. Leftovers from this recipe will keep in the refrigerator for up to 3 days.

½ cup light brown sugar

2 teaspoons cornstarch

⅛ teaspoon plus ½ teaspoon salt, divided

4 ounces crushed pineapple with syrup

2 tablespoons freshly squeezed lemon juice

1 tablespoon yellow mustard

1½ pounds raw large shrimp, peeled and deveined

2 eggs

½ cup all-purpose flour

1 cup unsweetened shredded coconut

¼ teaspoon granulated garlic

Olive oil spray

DAIRY FREE, FAMILY FAVORITE, FAST, NUT FREE

1. In a medium saucepan over medium heat, combine the brown sugar, cornstarch, and ⅛ teaspoon of salt.

2. As the brown sugar mixture melts into a sauce, stir in the crushed pineapple with syrup, lemon juice, and mustard. Cook for about 4 minutes until the mixture thickens and begins to boil. Boil for 1 minute. Remove the pan from the heat, set aside, and let cool while you make the shrimp.

3. Put the shrimp on a plate and pat them dry with paper towels.

4. In a small bowl, whisk the eggs.

5. In a medium bowl, stir together the flour, shredded coconut, remaining ½ teaspoon of salt, and granulated garlic.

6. Insert the crisper plate into the basket and the basket into the unit. Preheat the unit by selecting AIR FRY, setting the temperature to 400°F, and setting the time to 3 minutes. Select START/STOP to begin.

(continued)

Island Coconut Shrimp with Pineapple Sauce *continued*

7. Dip the shrimp into the egg and into the coconut mixture to coat.

8. Once the unit is preheated, place a parchment paper liner into the basket. Place the coated shrimp on the liner in a single layer and spray them with olive oil.

9. Select AIR FRY, set the temperature to 400ºF, and set the time to 13 minutes. Select START/STOP to begin.

10. After 6 minutes, remove the basket, flip the shrimp, and spray them with more olive oil. Reinsert the basket to resume cooking. Check the shrimp after 3 minutes more. If browned, they are done; if not, resume cooking.

11. When the cooking is complete, serve with the prepared pineapple sauce.

INGREDIENT TIP: For the fastest preparation, buy uncooked shrimp that are already shelled and deveined. If you choose to purchase unprepared shrimp, pull off the shells and the legs, leaving the shell on the tail. Run a knife along the back of the shrimp and rinse out the dark vein.

Per Serving: *Calories: 499; Total fat: 19g; Saturated fat: 13g; Cholesterol: 349mg; Sodium: 1007mg; Carbohydrates: 49g; Fiber: 3g; Protein: 41g*

Scallops and Spring Veggies

PREP TIME: 10 MINUTES / COOK TIME: 7 TO 10 MINUTES / SERVES 4 / 400°F / AIR FRY

Scallops cook in minutes, which makes them ideal for a quick dinner. When paired with bright green vegetables, they make an elegant meal. When you buy scallops, make sure you smell them first. They should smell fresh and of the sea.

Cooking oil spray

1 pound asparagus, ends trimmed, cut into 2-inch pieces

1 cup sugar snap peas

1 pound sea scallops

1 tablespoon freshly squeezed lemon juice

2 teaspoons extra-virgin olive oil

½ teaspoon dried thyme

Salt

Freshly ground black pepper

DAIRY FREE, FAST, GLUTEN FREE, NUT FREE

1. Insert the crisper plate into the basket and the basket into the unit. Preheat the unit by selecting AIR FRY, setting the temperature to 400°F, and setting the time to 3 minutes. Select START/STOP to begin.

2. Once the unit is preheated, spray the crisper plate with cooking oil. Place the asparagus and sugar snap peas into the basket.

3. Select AIR FRY, set the temperature to 400°F, and set the time to 10 minutes. Select START/STOP to begin.

4. Meanwhile, check the scallops for a small muscle attached to the side. Pull it off and discard. In a medium bowl, toss together the scallops, lemon juice, olive oil, and thyme. Season with salt and pepper.

5. After 3 minutes, the vegetables should be just starting to get tender. Place the scallops on top of the vegetables. Reinsert the basket to resume cooking. After 3 minutes more, remove the basket and shake it. Again reinsert the basket to resume cooking.

6. When the cooking is complete, the scallops should be firm when tested with your finger and opaque in the center, and the vegetables tender. Serve immediately.

Per Serving: Calories: 159; Total fat: 4g; Saturated fat: <1g; Cholesterol: 37mg; Sodium: 187mg; Carbohydrates: 11g; Fiber: 3g; Protein: 22g

AIR FRYER TIP: If you have an air fryer that comes with a wire rack, use it to make this meal even faster. Cook the scallops on the rack above the vegetables for 5 to 6 minutes until done.

Crab Cakes

PREP TIME: 5 MINUTES / COOK TIME: 10 MINUTES / SERVES 4 / 375°F / AIR FRY

Crab cakes work well as both an appetizer and a main dish. In the air fryer, this satisfying recipe flavored with classic Old Bay takes only 15 minutes to prepare and cook! Serve alone or on a bun with mayo and lettuce to create a crab cake sandwich.

8 ounces jumbo lump crabmeat

1 tablespoon Old Bay seasoning

⅓ cup bread crumbs

¼ cup diced red bell pepper

¼ cup diced green bell pepper

1 egg

¼ cup mayonnaise

Juice of ½ lemon

1 teaspoon all-purpose flour

Cooking oil spray

DAIRY FREE, FAMILY FAVORITE, FAST, NUT FREE

1. Sort through the crabmeat, picking out any bits of shell or cartilage.

2. In a large bowl, stir together the Old Bay seasoning, bread crumbs, red and green bell peppers, egg, mayonnaise, and lemon juice. Gently stir in the crabmeat.

3. Insert the crisper plate into the basket and the basket into the unit. Preheat the unit by selecting AIR FRY, setting the temperature to 375°F, and setting the time to 3 minutes. Select START/STOP to begin.

4. Form the mixture into 4 patties. Sprinkle ¼ teaspoon of flour on top of each patty.

5. Once the unit is preheated, spray the crisper plate with cooking oil. Place the crab cakes into the basket and spray them with cooking oil.

6. Select AIR FRY, set the temperature to 375°F, and set the time to 10 minutes. Select START/STOP to begin.

7. When the cooking is complete, the crab cakes will be golden brown and firm.

Per Serving: *Calories: 176; Total fat: 8g; Saturated fat: 1g; Cholesterol: 101mg; Sodium: 826mg; Carbohydrates: 12g; Fiber: 1g; Protein: 15g*

INGREDIENT TIP: You can make your own crab seasoning using ¼ teaspoon each of celery salt, black pepper, red pepper flakes, and paprika. To make more and store it for future use, use 2 tablespoons of each ingredient and store in an airtight container for up to 1 month.

Chicken Fajitas,
page 120

7

Poultry Mains

Chicken Fajitas

PREP TIME: 10 MINUTES / COOK TIME: 10 TO 14 MINUTES / SERVES 4 / 375°F / BAKE

Fajitas are a delicious Tex-Mex dish, made with grilled chicken and veggies, tossed with a spicy dressing, and served with avocados and lettuce in a soft corn tortilla. You can adjust the heat of this dish with the spice level of the dressing or salsa you choose.

Cooking oil spray

4 boneless, skinless chicken breasts, sliced crosswise

1 small red onion, sliced

2 red bell peppers, seeded and sliced

½ cup spicy ranch salad dressing, divided

½ teaspoon dried oregano

8 corn tortillas

2 cups torn butter lettuce leaves

2 avocados, peeled, pitted, and chopped

FAMILY FAVORITE, FAST, GLUTEN FREE, NUT FREE

SUBSTITUTION TIP: You could use sliced boneless, skinless chicken thighs instead of the chicken breasts. The cooking time will be a bit longer—12 to 17 minutes. Make sure you check the doneness with a food thermometer; all chicken should be cooked to 165°F.

1. Insert the crisper plate into the basket and the basket into the unit. Preheat the unit by selecting BAKE, setting the temperature to 375°F, and setting the time to 3 minutes. Select START/STOP to begin.

2. Once the unit is preheated, spray the crisper plate with cooking oil. Place the chicken, red onion, and red bell pepper into the basket. Drizzle with 1 tablespoon of the salad dressing and season with the oregano. Toss to combine.

3. Select BAKE, set the temperature to 375°F, and set the time to 14 minutes. Select START/STOP to begin.

4. After 10 minutes, check the chicken. If a food thermometer inserted into the chicken registers at least 165°F, it is done. If not, resume cooking.

5. When the cooking is complete, transfer the chicken and vegetables to a bowl and toss with the remaining salad dressing.

6. Serve the chicken mixture family-style with the tortillas, lettuce, and avocados, and let everyone make their own plates.

Per Serving: *Calories: 783; Total fat: 38g; Saturated fat: 9g; Cholesterol: 202mg; Sodium: 397mg; Carbohydrates: 39g; Fiber: 12g; Protein 62g*

Warm Chicken and Spinach Salad

PREP TIME: 10 MINUTES / COOK TIME: 20 MINUTES / SERVES 4 / 375°F / AIR ROAST

This salad is similar to the wilted spinach salads popular in the 1980s, but it is much healthier. There's no bacon, for instance, and the dressing is made from healthy olive oil and lemon juice instead of bacon drippings. Still, this satisfying light lunch or dinner is packed with flavor and is easy to prepare on a busy weeknight.

3 (5-ounce) boneless, skinless chicken breasts, cut into 1-inch cubes

5 teaspoons extra-virgin olive oil

½ teaspoon dried thyme

1 medium red onion, sliced

1 red bell pepper, sliced

1 small zucchini, cut into strips

3 tablespoons freshly squeezed lemon juice

6 cups fresh baby spinach leaves

DAIRY FREE, FAMILY FAVORITE, FAST, GLUTEN FREE, NUT FREE

1. Insert the crisper plate into the basket and the basket into the unit. Preheat the unit by selecting AIR ROAST, setting the temperature to 375ºF, and setting the time to 3 minutes. Select START/STOP to begin.

2. In a large bowl, combine the chicken, olive oil, and thyme. Toss to coat. Transfer to a medium metal bowl that fits into the basket.

3. Once the unit is preheated, place the bowl into the basket.

4. Select AIR ROAST, set the temperature to 375ºF, and set the time to 20 minutes. Select START/STOP to begin.

5. After 8 minutes, add the red onion, red bell pepper, and zucchini to the bowl. Resume cooking. After about 6 minutes more, stir the chicken and vegetables. Resume cooking.

(continued)

Warm Chicken and Spinach Salad *continued*

6. When the cooking is complete, a food thermometer inserted into the chicken should register at least 165°F. Remove the bowl from the unit and stir in the lemon juice.

7. Put the spinach in a serving bowl and top with the chicken mixture. Toss to combine and serve immediately.

Per Serving: Calories: 190; Total fat: 8g; Saturated fat: 1g; Cholesterol: 61mg; Sodium: 222mg; Carbohydrates: 8g; Fiber: 3g; Protein: 24g

SUBSTITUTION TIP: You could use other greens in place of the baby spinach. Use a combination of romaine lettuce and kale, or try kale and spinach. Experiment to find the combination you like best. You could also cook other veggies. Try sliced yellow summer squash in place of the zucchini.

Spicy Chicken Meatballs

PREP TIME: 10 MINUTES / COOK TIME: 25 MINUTES / SERVES 4 / 400°F / BAKE

Meatballs made with ground chicken are lighter and more tender than the typical meatball made with beef or pork. If you like things spicy, double the jalapeño pepper and add some red pepper flakes. Serve these as an appetizer, light lunch, or quick dinner. You can mix the finished meatballs with heated marinara sauce and serve over hot cooked pasta.

1 medium red onion, minced

2 garlic cloves, minced

1 jalapeño pepper, minced

2 teaspoons extra-virgin olive oil

3 tablespoons ground almonds

1 egg

1 teaspoon dried thyme

1 pound ground chicken breast

Cooking oil spray

DAIRY FREE, FAMILY FAVORITE, GLUTEN FREE

1. Insert the crisper plate into the basket and the basket into the unit. Preheat the unit by selecting BAKE, setting the temperature to 400ºF, and setting the time to 3 minutes. Select START/STOP to begin.

2. In a 6-by-2-inch round pan, combine the red onion, garlic, jalapeño, and olive oil.

3. Once the unit is preheated, place the pan into the basket.

4. Select BAKE, set the temperature to 400ºF, and set the time to 4 minutes. Select START/STOP to begin.

5. When the cooking is complete, the vegetables should be crisp-tender. Transfer to a medium bowl.

6. Mix the almonds, egg, and thyme into the vegetable mixture. Add the chicken and mix until just combined. Form the chicken mixture into about 24 (1-inch) balls.

7. Insert the crisper plate into the basket and the basket into the unit. Preheat the unit by selecting BAKE, setting the temperature to 400ºF, and setting the time to 3 minutes. Select START/STOP to begin.

(continued)

Spicy Chicken Meatballs *continued*

8. Once the unit is preheated, spray the crisper plate with cooking oil. Working in batches, place half the meatballs in a single layer, not touching, into the basket.

9. Select BAKE, set the temperature to 400ºF, and set the time to 10 minutes. Select START/STOP to begin.

10. When the cooking is complete, a food thermometer inserted into the meatballs should register at least 165ºF.

11. Repeat steps 8 and 9 with the remaining meatballs. Serve warm.

VARIATION TIP: For a nut-free chicken meatball, omit the ground almonds and use whole-wheat bread crumbs instead. Of course, that means the meatballs won't be gluten-free, so if you need to, substitute gluten-free bread crumbs.

Per Serving *(6 meatballs): Calories: 187; Total fat: 7g; Saturated fat: 1g; Cholesterol: 116mg; Sodium: 79mg; Carbohydrates: 5g; Fiber: 2g; Protein: 28g*

Italian Chicken Parmesan

PREP TIME: 10 MINUTES / COOK TIME: 20 MINUTES / SERVES 4 / 375°F / AIR FRY

Goodbye, deep-fried chicken; hello, crunchy air fryer chicken cutlets. This recipe may become your go-to dinner on weeknights when time is scarce and you have an entire family to feed. The combination of melted mozzarella cheese and crunchy breading in this recipe is irresistible.

2 (4-ounce) boneless, skinless chicken breasts

2 egg whites, beaten

1 cup Italian bread crumbs

½ cup grated Parmesan cheese

2 teaspoons Italian seasoning

Salt

Freshly ground black pepper

Cooking oil spray

¾ cup marinara sauce

½ cup shredded mozzarella cheese

FAMILY FAVORITE, FAST, NUT FREE

1. With your knife blade parallel to the cutting board, cut the chicken breasts in half horizontally to create 4 thin cutlets. On a solid surface, pound the cutlets to flatten them. You can use your hands, a rolling pin, a kitchen mallet, or a meat hammer.

2. Pour the egg whites into a bowl large enough to dip the chicken.

3. In another bowl large enough to dip a chicken cutlet in, stir together the bread crumbs, Parmesan cheese, and Italian seasoning, and season with salt and pepper.

4. Dip each cutlet into the egg whites and into the bread-crumb mixture to coat.

5. Insert the crisper plate into the basket and the basket into the unit. Preheat the unit by selecting AIR FRY, setting the temperature to 375ºF, and setting the time to 3 minutes. Select START/STOP to begin.

(continued)

Italian Chicken Parmesan *continued*

6. Once the unit is preheated, spray the crisper plate with cooking oil. Working in batches, place 2 chicken cutlets into the basket. Spray the top of the chicken with cooking oil.

7. Select AIR FRY, set the temperature to 375°F, and set the time to 7 minutes. Select START/STOP to begin.

8. When the cooking is complete, repeat steps 6 and 7 with the remaining cutlets.

9. Top the chicken cutlets with the marinara sauce and shredded mozzarella cheese. If the chicken will fit into the basket without stacking, you can prepare all 4 at once. Otherwise, do this 2 cutlets at a time.

10. Select AIR FRY, set the temperature to 375°F, and set the time to 3 minutes. Select START/STOP to begin.

11. The cooking is complete when the cheese is melted and the chicken reaches an internal temperature of 165°F. Cool for 5 minutes before serving.

COOKING TIP: Preparing this dish in batches yields the best results because the chicken has room around it for the hot air to circulate, allowing it to nicely crisp and brown. The cook time for this recipe (20 minutes) is for cooking the chicken cutlets in two batches.

Per Serving: *Calories: 257; Total fat: 8g; Saturated fat: 3g; Cholesterol: 46mg; Sodium: 593mg; Carbohydrates: 23g; Fiber: 1g; Protein: 24g*

Easy General Tso's Chicken

PREP TIME: 10 MINUTES / COOK TIME: 14 MINUTES / SERVES 4 / 400°F / BAKE

If you love to live life on the spicy side, this takeout classic answers the call. This easy recipe is finished with a zesty sauce that's sure to grab your attention. Serve it with steamed broccoli or carrots on the side, or a crisp green salad.

1 tablespoon sesame oil

1 teaspoon minced garlic

½ teaspoon ground ginger

1 cup chicken broth

4 tablespoons soy sauce, divided

½ teaspoon sriracha, plus more for serving

2 tablespoons hoisin sauce

4 tablespoons cornstarch, divided

4 boneless, skinless chicken breasts, cut into 1-inch pieces

Olive oil spray

2 medium scallions, sliced, green parts only

Sesame seeds, for garnish

DAIRY FREE, FAST, NUT FREE

1. In a small saucepan over low heat, combine the sesame oil, garlic, and ginger and cook for 1 minute.

2. Add the chicken broth, 2 tablespoons of soy sauce, the sriracha, and hoisin. Whisk to combine.

3. Whisk in 2 tablespoons of cornstarch and continue cooking over low heat until the sauce starts to thicken, about 5 minutes. Remove the pan from the heat, cover it, and set aside.

4. Insert the crisper plate into the basket and the basket into the unit. Preheat the unit by selecting BAKE, setting the temperature to 400°F, and setting the time to 3 minutes. Select START/STOP to begin.

5. In a medium bowl, toss together the chicken, remaining 2 tablespoons of soy sauce, and remaining 2 tablespoons of cornstarch.

6. Once the unit is preheated, spray the crisper plate with olive oil. Place the chicken into the basket and spray it with olive oil.

(continued)

Easy General Tso's Chicken *continued*

7. Select BAKE, set the temperature to 400°F, and set the time to 9 minutes. Select START/STOP to begin.

8. After 5 minutes, remove the basket, shake, and spray the chicken with more olive oil. Reinsert the basket to resume cooking.

9. When the cooking is complete, a food thermometer inserted into the chicken should register at least 165°F. Transfer the chicken to a large bowl and toss it with the sauce. Garnish with the scallions and sesame seeds and serve.

Per Serving *(1 chicken breast): Calories: 205; Total fat: 7g; Saturated fat: 1g; Cholesterol: 66mg; Sodium: 1,465mg; Carbohydrates: 13g; Fiber: 1g; Protein: 25g*

VARIATION TIP: You can use boneless, skinless chicken thighs instead of chicken breasts (look for them next to the chicken tenders at your grocer). Cut them into pieces before cooking. The thighs will cook for 1 to 2 minutes longer. Feel free to add some dried red chile peppers if you like to heat it up even more. You can also add 1 teaspoon of red pepper flakes.

Spicy Coconut Chicken Wings

PREP TIME: 15 MINUTES, PLUS 30 MINUTES TO MARINATE / COOK TIME: 20 MINUTES /
SERVES 4 / 400°F / AIR FRY

*Pair these spicy and sweet chicken wings with mango salsa and coconut rice for a picture
of paradise. They are crunchy, sweet, savory, and delicious. You will need a resealable
plastic bag for this recipe.*

**16 chicken drumettes
(party wings)**

¼ cup full-fat coconut milk

1 tablespoon sriracha

1 teaspoon onion powder

1 teaspoon garlic powder

Salt

Freshly ground black pepper

**⅓ cup shredded
unsweetened coconut**

½ cup all-purpose flour

Cooking oil spray

**1 cup mango, cut into
½-inch chunks**

**¼ cup fresh
cilantro, chopped**

½ cup red onion, chopped

2 garlic cloves, minced

Juice of ½ lime

DAIRY FREE, FAMILY
FAVORITE

1. Place the drumettes in a resealable plastic bag.

2. In a small bowl, whisk the coconut milk and sriracha.

3. Drizzle the drumettes with the sriracha–coconut milk
mixture. Season the drumettes with the onion powder, garlic
powder, salt, and pepper. Seal the bag. Shake it thoroughly to
combine the seasonings and coat the chicken. Marinate for at
least 30 minutes, preferably overnight, in the refrigerator.

4. When the drumettes are almost done marinating, in a
large bowl, stir together the shredded coconut and flour.

5. Dip the drumettes into the coconut-flour mixture. Press
the flour mixture onto the chicken with your hands.

6. Insert the crisper plate into the basket and the basket into
the unit. Preheat the unit by selecting AIR FRY, setting the
temperature to 400°F, and setting the time to 3 minutes.
Select START/STOP to begin.

(continued)

Spicy Coconut Chicken Wings *continued*

7. Once the unit is preheated, spray the crisper plate and the basket with cooking oil. Place the drumettes in the air fryer. It is okay to stack them. Spray the drumettes with cooking oil, being sure to cover the bottom layer.

8. Select AIR FRY, set the temperature to 400ºF, and set the time to 20 minutes. Select START/STOP to begin.

9. After 5 minutes, remove the basket and shake it to ensure all pieces cook through. Reinsert the basket to resume cooking. Remove and shake the basket every 5 minutes, twice more, until a food thermometer inserted into the drumettes registers 165ºF.

10. When the cooking is complete, let the chicken cool for 5 minutes.

11. While the chicken cooks and cools, make the salsa. In a small bowl, combine the mango, cilantro, red onion, garlic, and lime juice. Mix well until fully combined. Serve with the wings.

PREPARATION TIP: Make sure the coconut-flour mixture is pressed onto the chicken wings before you put them into the air fryer basket. If you don't, the coconut could fly around in the air fryer and burn.

Per Serving: *Calories: 375; Total fat: 15g; Saturated fat: 6g; Cholesterol: 160mg; Sodium: 257mg; Carbohydrates: 14g; Fiber: 1g; Protein: 46g*

Chili Ranch Chicken Wings

PREP TIME: 10 MINUTES, PLUS 30 MINUTES TO MARINATE / COOK TIME: 40 MINUTES
SERVES 4 / 400°F / AIR FRY

This version of chicken wings is spicy and cool and very easy to make using ingredients you can find at any grocery store. You don't need a dipping sauce, but if you'd like one, use a combination of ranch dressing and mayonnaise.

---

2 tablespoons water

2 tablespoons hot pepper sauce

2 tablespoons unsalted butter, melted

2 tablespoons apple cider vinegar

1 (1-ounce) envelope ranch salad dressing mix

1 teaspoon paprika

4 pounds chicken wings, tips removed

Cooking oil spray

GLUTEN FREE, NUT FREE

1. In a large bowl, whisk the water, hot pepper sauce, melted butter, vinegar, salad dressing mix, and paprika until combined.

2. Add the wings and toss to coat. At this point, you can cover the bowl and marinate the wings in the refrigerator for 4 to 24 hours for best results. However, you can just let the wings stand for 30 minutes in the refrigerator.

3. Insert the crisper plate into the basket and the basket into the unit. Preheat the unit by selecting AIR FRY, setting the temperature to 400ºF, and setting the time to 3 minutes. Select START/STOP to begin.

4. Once the unit is preheated, spray the crisper plate with cooking oil. Working in batches, put half the wings into the basket; it is okay to stack them. Refrigerate the remaining wings.

5. Select AIR FRY, set the temperature to 400ºF, and set the time to 20 minutes. Select START/STOP to begin.

(continued)

Chili Ranch Chicken Wings *continued*

6. After 5 minutes, remove the basket and shake it. Reinsert the basket to resume cooking. Remove and shake the basket every 5 minutes, three more times, until the chicken is browned and glazed and a food thermometer inserted into the wings registers 165°F.

7. Repeat steps 4, 5, and 6 with the remaining wings.

8. When the cooking is complete, serve warm.

Per Serving: *Calories 953; Total fat: 70g; Saturated fat: 22g; Cholesterol: 335mg; Sodium: 1527mg; Carbohydrates: 4g; Fiber: 0g; Protein: 76g*

SUBSTITUTION TIP: You can use any flavor of dry salad dressing mix in this easy and flavorful recipe. Try Italian, garlic and herb, or spicy ranch. Reduce the quantity of the hot sauce if you want a milder recipe.

Crispy Chicken Thighs with Roasted Carrots

PREP TIME: 10 MINUTES / COOK TIME: 22 MINUTES / SERVES 4 / 400°F / AIR FRY

Chicken thighs are a favorite because they are inexpensive but full of flavor. The key to this recipe is using bone-in, skin-on chicken thighs. The skin keeps the meat moist and the bone adds lots of flavor. Say so long to rubbery chicken skin and hello to caramelized perfection! The carrots caramelize, too, developing the most wonderful crisp-tender texture.

4 bone-in, skin-on chicken thighs

2 carrots, cut into 2-inch pieces

2 tablespoons extra-virgin olive oil

2 teaspoons poultry spice

1 teaspoon sea salt, divided

2 teaspoons chopped fresh rosemary leaves

Cooking oil spray

2 cups cooked white rice

DAIRY FREE, FAMILY FAVORITE, NUT FREE

1. Brush the chicken thighs and carrots with olive oil. Sprinkle both with the poultry spice, salt, and rosemary.

2. Insert the crisper plate into the basket and the basket into the unit. Preheat the unit by selecting AIR FRY, setting the temperature to 400°F, and setting the time to 3 minutes. Select START/STOP to begin.

3. Once the unit is preheated, spray the crisper plate with cooking oil. Place the carrots into the basket. Add the wire rack and arrange the chicken thighs on the rack.

4. Select AIR FRY, set the temperature to 400°F, and set the time to 20 minutes. Select START/STOP to begin.

5. When the cooking is complete, check the chicken temperature. If a food thermometer inserted into the chicken registers 165°F, remove the chicken from the air fryer, place it on a clean plate, and cover with aluminum foil to keep warm. Otherwise, resume cooking for 1 to 2 minutes longer.

(continued)

Crispy Chicken Thighs with Roasted Carrots *continued*

6. The carrots can cook for 18 to 22 minutes and will be tender and caramelized; cooking time isn't as crucial for root vegetables.

7. Serve the chicken and carrots with the hot cooked rice.

SUBSTITUTION TIP: Try other veggies, like chopped parsnips or sweet potatoes, in this easy recipe. You can use other herbs, too; try fresh thyme or oregano.

Per Serving: Calories 425; Total fat: 18g; Saturated fat: 4g; Cholesterol: 51mg; Sodium: 761mg; Carbohydrates: 48g; Fiber: 6g; Protein: 18g

Buffalo Chicken Strips

PREP TIME: 15 MINUTES / COOK TIME: 13 TO 17 MINUTES PER BATCH / SERVES 4 / 375°F / AIR FRY

You no longer need to head to the corner pub for good food while you support your team—these Buffalo strips are the perfect game-day snack. Crunchy chicken breasts smothered in spicy Buffalo sauce are spicy, tender, and delicious. Serve with the classics—sides of blue cheese dressing, carrots, and celery—for the full experience.

¾ cup all-purpose flour

2 eggs

2 tablespoons water

1 cup seasoned panko bread crumbs

2 teaspoons granulated garlic

1 teaspoon salt

1 teaspoon freshly ground black pepper

16 chicken breast strips, or 3 large boneless, skinless chicken breasts, cut into 1-inch strips

Olive oil spray

¼ cup Buffalo sauce, plus more as needed (or see Substitution Tip)

FAMILY FAVORITE, NUT FREE

1. Put the flour in a small bowl.

2. In another small bowl, whisk the eggs and the water.

3. In a third bowl, stir together the panko, granulated garlic, salt, and pepper.

4. Dip each chicken strip in the flour, in the egg, and in the panko mixture to coat. Press the crumbs onto the chicken with your fingers.

5. Insert the crisper plate into the basket and the basket into the unit. Preheat the unit by selecting AIR FRY, setting the temperature to 375ºF, and setting the time to 3 minutes. Select START/STOP to begin.

6. Once the unit is preheated, place a parchment paper liner into the basket. Working in batches if needed, place the chicken strips into the basket. Do not stack unless using a wire rack for the second layer. Spray the top of the chicken with olive oil.

(continued)

Buffalo Chicken Strips *continued*

7. Select AIR FRY, set the temperature to 375°F, and set the time to 17 minutes. Select START/STOP to begin.

8. After 10 or 12 minutes, remove the basket, flip the chicken, and spray again with olive oil. Reinsert the basket to resume cooking.

9. When the cooking is complete, the chicken should be golden brown and crispy and a food thermometer inserted into the chicken should register 165°F.

10. Repeat steps 6, 7, and 8 with any remaining chicken.

11. Transfer the chicken to a large bowl. Drizzle the Buffalo sauce over the top of the cooked chicken, toss to coat, and serve.

Per Serving (4 strips): Calories: 320; Total fat: 6g; Saturated fat: 2g; Cholesterol: 203mg; Sodium: 1910mg; Carbohydrates: 36g; Fiber: 2g; Protein: 30g

INGREDIENT TIP: You can buy boneless, skinless chicken breasts and slice your own strips to save money. Or, if you are looking for convenience, precut chicken strips are widely available, fresh or frozen, making prep time super quick.

SUBSTITUTION TIP: You can make your own Buffalo sauce. Just whisk together ⅓ cup melted salted butter, ⅓ cup hot sauce, 1 tablespoon white vinegar, 1 teaspoon Worcestershire sauce, ⅛ teaspoon cayenne, ⅛ teaspoon paprika, and ⅛ teaspoon garlic powder. Refrigerate in an airtight container up to 1 week.

Chicken Satay

PREP TIME: 12 MINUTES / COOK TIME: 12 TO 18 MINUTES / SERVES 4 / 390°F / AIR FRY

Satay is a delicious Indonesian dish made of meat, usually chicken, that is skewered and grilled with a spicy peanut sauce. The tender grilled skewers are then served with additional peanut sauce for dipping.

½ cup crunchy peanut butter

⅓ cup chicken broth

3 tablespoons low-sodium soy sauce

2 tablespoons freshly squeezed lemon juice

2 garlic cloves, minced

2 tablespoons extra-virgin olive oil

1 teaspoon curry powder

1 pound chicken tenders

Cooking oil spray

DAIRY FREE, FAMILY FAVORITE, FAST

1. In a medium bowl, whisk the peanut butter, broth, soy sauce, lemon juice, garlic, olive oil, and curry powder until smooth.

2. Place 2 tablespoons of this mixture into a small bowl. Transfer the remaining sauce to a serving bowl and set aside.

3. Add the chicken tenders to the bowl with the 2 tablespoons of sauce and stir to coat. Let stand for a few minutes to marinate.

4. Insert the crisper plate into the basket and the basket into the unit. Preheat the unit by selecting AIR FRY, setting the temperature to 390ºF, and setting the time to 3 minutes. Select START/STOP to begin.

5. Run a 6-inch bamboo skewer lengthwise through each chicken tender.

6. Once the unit is preheated, spray the crisper plate with cooking oil. Working in batches, place half the chicken skewers into the basket in a single layer without overlapping.

7. Select AIR FRY, set the temperature to 390ºF, and set the time to 9 minutes. Select START/STOP to begin.

(continued)

Chicken Satay *continued*

8. After 6 minutes, check the chicken. If a food thermometer inserted into the chicken registers 165ºF, it is done. If not, resume cooking.

9. Repeat steps 6, 7, and 8 with the remaining chicken.

10. When the cooking is complete, serve the chicken with the reserved sauce.

AIR FRYER TIP: The air fryer may smoke a bit as some of the sauce drips off the chicken. You can add 1 to 2 tablespoons of water to the pan attached to the basket if you'd like to reduce the smoke.

Per Serving: *Calories: 448; Total fat: 28g; Saturated fat: 5g; Cholesterol: 97mg; Sodium: 1,004mg; Carbohydrates: 8g; Fiber: 2g; Protein: 46g*

Crispy Chicken Tenders

PREP TIME: 10 MINUTES / COOK TIME: 15 MINUTES / SERVES 4 / 350°F / AIR FRY

Crispy chicken tenders are a dinnertime win. These panko-coated strips are generously seasoned and air fried until they're crunchy on the outside—but still tender and juicy on the inside. Dipped in your favorite sauce, or alongside a bowl of your favorite soup, these chicken tenders let you get a delicious protein-rich dish on the table in minutes.

1 cup panko bread crumbs
1 tablespoon paprika
½ teaspoon salt
¼ teaspoon freshly ground black pepper

16 chicken tenders
½ cup mayonnaise
Olive oil spray

DAIRY FREE, FAMILY FAVORITE, FAST, NUT FREE

1. In a medium bowl, stir together the panko, paprika, salt, and pepper.

2. In a large bowl, toss together the chicken tenders and mayonnaise to coat. Transfer the coated chicken pieces to the bowl of seasoned panko and dredge to coat thoroughly. Press the coating onto the chicken with your fingers.

3. Insert the crisper plate into the basket and the basket into the unit. Preheat the unit by selecting AIR FRY, setting the temperature to 350ºF, and setting the time to 3 minutes. Select START/STOP to begin.

4. Once the unit is preheated, place a parchment paper liner into the basket. Place the chicken into the basket and spray it with olive oil.

5. Select AIR FRY, set the temperature to 350ºF, and set the time to 15 minutes. Select START/STOP to begin.

(continued)

Crispy Chicken Tenders *continued*

6. When the cooking is complete, the tenders will be golden brown and a food thermometer inserted into the chicken should register 165°F. For more even browning, remove the basket halfway through cooking and flip the tenders. Give them an extra spray of olive oil and reinsert the basket to resume cooking. This ensures they are crispy and brown all over.

7. When the cooking is complete, serve.

SUBSTITUTION TIP: If you can't find panko bread crumbs, you can make your own. Crumble whole-wheat bread into coarse crumbs and place on a baking sheet. Bake in a preheated 325°F oven for 4 to 6 minutes, stirring once during the baking time, until the crumbs are deep golden brown and crisp.

Per Serving (4 tenders): Calories: 377; Total fat: 22g; Saturated fat: 3g; Cholesterol: 73mg; Sodium: 799mg; Carbohydrates: 18g; Fiber: 1g; Protein: 28g

Chicken Cordon Bleu

PREP TIME: 15 MINUTES / COOK TIME: 15 MINUTES / SERVES 4 / 375°F / BAKE

Cordon bleu *is French for "blue ribbon," and Le Cordon Bleu is the name of the famous cooking school in Paris. Chicken Cordon Bleu is chicken stuffed with ham and Swiss or Gruyère cheese. It's a delicious and fancy recipe that's a cinch to make with the air fryer.*

4 chicken breast filets

¼ cup chopped ham

⅓ cup grated Swiss cheese, or Gruyère cheese

¼ cup all-purpose flour

Pinch salt

Freshly ground black pepper

½ teaspoon dried marjoram

1 egg

1 cup panko bread crumbs

Olive oil spray

DAIRY FREE, FAMILY FAVORITE, FAST, NUT FREE

1. Put the chicken breast filets on a work surface and gently press them with the palm of your hand to make them a bit thinner. Don't tear the meat.

2. In a small bowl, combine the ham and cheese. Divide this mixture among the chicken filets. Wrap the chicken around the filling to enclose it, using toothpicks to hold the chicken together.

3. In a shallow bowl, stir together the flour, salt, pepper, and marjoram.

4. In another bowl, beat the egg.

5. Spread the panko on a plate.

6. Dip the chicken in the flour mixture, in the egg, and in the panko to coat thoroughly. Press the crumbs into the chicken so they stick well.

7. Insert the crisper plate into the basket and the basket into the unit. Preheat the unit by selecting BAKE, setting the temperature to 375ºF, and setting the time to 3 minutes. Select START/STOP to begin.

(continued)

Chicken Cordon Bleu *continued*

8. Once the unit is preheated, spray the crisper plate with olive oil. Place the chicken into the basket and spray it with olive oil.

9. Select BAKE, set the temperature to 375ºF, and set the time to 15 minutes. Select START/STOP to begin.

10. When the cooking is complete, the chicken should be cooked through and a food thermometer inserted into the chicken should register 165ºF. Carefully remove the tooth-picks and serve.

Per Serving: *Calories: 478; Total fat: 12g; Saturated fat: 3g; Cholesterol: 200mg; Sodium: 575mg; Carbohydrates: 26g; Fiber: 2g; Protein: 64g*

INGREDIENT TIP: You can find chicken filets, which are cut from the chicken breast, in most large grocery stores. If you can't find them, you can cut one chicken breast in half, holding your knife parallel to the work surface, to make two thin slices.

Spicy Air-Crisped Chicken and Potatoes

PREP TIME: 5 MINUTES / COOK TIME: 25 MINUTES / SERVES 4 / 400°F / AIR FRY

It's really nice to cook your main dish and a side dish in the air fryer at the same time; you can do it by using an air fryer rack. The chicken cooks on top of the potatoes, dripping wonderful flavor onto the spuds. Serve this recipe with a nice green salad tossed with some mushrooms and ranch dressing.

4 bone-in, skin-on chicken thighs

½ teaspoon kosher salt or ¼ teaspoon fine salt

2 tablespoons melted unsalted butter

2 teaspoons Worcestershire sauce

2 teaspoons curry powder

1 teaspoon dried oregano leaves

½ teaspoon dry mustard

½ teaspoon granulated garlic

¼ teaspoon paprika

¼ teaspoon hot pepper sauce, such as Tabasco

Cooking oil spray

4 medium Yukon gold potatoes, chopped

1 tablespoon extra-virgin olive oil

FAMILY FAVORITE, FAST, GLUTEN FREE, NUT FREE

1. Sprinkle the chicken thighs on both sides with salt.

2. In a medium bowl, stir together the melted butter, Worcestershire sauce, curry powder, oregano, dry mustard, granulated garlic, paprika, and hot pepper sauce. Add the thighs to the sauce and stir to coat.

3. Insert the crisper plate into the basket and the basket into the unit. Preheat the unit by selecting AIR FRY, setting the temperature to 400°F, and setting the time to 3 minutes. Select START/STOP to begin.

4. Once the unit is preheated, spray the crisper plate with cooking oil. In the basket, combine the potatoes and olive oil and toss to coat.

5. Add the wire rack to the air fryer and place the chicken thighs on top.

(continued)

Spicy Air-Crisped Chicken and Potatoes *continued*

6. Select AIR FRY, set the temperature to 400°F, and set the time to 25 minutes. Select START/STOP to begin.

7. After 19 minutes check the chicken thighs. If a food thermometer inserted into the chicken registers 165°F, transfer them to a clean plate, and cover with aluminum foil to keep warm. If they aren't cooked to 165°F, resume cooking for another 1 to 2 minutes until they are done. Remove them from the unit along with the rack.

8. Remove the basket and shake it to distribute the potatoes. Reinsert the basket to resume cooking for 3 to 6 minutes, or until the potatoes are crisp and golden brown.

9. When the cooking is complete, serve the chicken with the potatoes.

SUBSTITUTION TIP: You can make this recipe with boneless, skinless chicken breasts or chicken tenders. Just keep in mind that the chicken breasts will cook in about 15 minutes, whereas the tenders will cook in 10 to 15 minutes. Use your food thermometer to make sure the chicken is perfectly cooked.

Per Serving: *Calories: 333; Total fat: 14g; Saturated fat: 5g; Cholesterol: 109mg; Sodium: 428mg; Carbohydrates: 27g; Fiber: 3g; Protein: 25g*

Buttermilk Fried Chicken

PREP TIME: 7 MINUTES / COOK TIME: 20 TO 25 MINUTES / SERVES 4 / 375°F / AIR FRY

Fried chicken is, perhaps, the most decadent of fried foods. But many people don't make it at home because oil often splatters everywhere when you fry chicken. And it's just not healthy to eat it too often. The air fryer comes to the rescue with this wonderful adaptation of crisp and tender fried chicken.

1 cup all-purpose flour

2 teaspoons paprika

Pinch salt

Freshly ground black pepper

⅓ cup buttermilk

2 eggs

2 tablespoons extra-virgin olive oil

1½ cups bread crumbs

6 chicken pieces, drumsticks, breasts, and thighs, patted dry

Cooking oil spray

FAMILY FAVORITE, NUT FREE

1. In a shallow bowl, stir together the flour, paprika, salt, and pepper.

2. In another bowl, beat the buttermilk and eggs until smooth.

3. In a third bowl, stir together the olive oil and bread crumbs until mixed.

4. Dredge the chicken in the flour, dip in the eggs to coat, and finally press into the bread crumbs, patting the crumbs firmly onto the chicken skin.

5. Insert the crisper plate into the basket and the basket into the unit. Preheat the unit by selecting AIR FRY, setting the temperature to 375°F, and setting the time to 3 minutes. Select START/STOP to begin.

6. Once the unit is preheated, spray the crisper plate with cooking oil. Place the chicken into the basket.

7. Select AIR FRY, set the temperature to 375°F, and set the time to 25 minutes. Select START/STOP to begin.

(continued)

Buttermilk Fried Chicken *continued*

8. After 10 minutes, flip the chicken. Resume cooking. After 10 minutes more, check the chicken. If a food thermometer inserted into the chicken registers 165ºF and the chicken is brown and crisp, it is done. Otherwise, resume cooking for up to 5 minutes longer.

9. When the cooking is complete, let cool for 5 minutes, then serve.

Per Serving: Calories: 644; Total fat: 17g; Saturated fat: 4g; Cholesterol: 214mg; Sodium: 495mg; Carbohydrates: 55g; Fiber: 3g; Protein: 62g

SUBSTITUTION TIP: You can marinate the chicken in buttermilk and spices, such as cayenne, chili powder, or garlic powder, in the refrigerator overnight before you cook it. This makes the chicken even more moist and tender and adds flavor.

VARIATION TIP: Boneless buttermilk fried chicken makes an excellent sandwich, too, topped with a simple coleslaw. To make the coleslaw, thinly slice ½ head green or red cabbage (or a combination) or use a prepackaged coleslaw blend. Next add ¼ cup mayonnaise, 1 tablespoon apple cider vinegar, and 1 tablespoon sugar or honey. Mix with the cabbage until well combined. Season with salt and pepper. Set aside, stirring occasionally, for at least 10 minutes before serving.

Korean Chicken Wings

These wings have a tangy, savory flavor because they are made with gochujang, a fermented red pepper paste. You can find red pepper paste at most big box grocers along with other savory spreads. Gochujang can be ordered online, too. These wings work equally well as a main dish paired with zucchini fries (see the Veggie Fries entry in No Recipe? No Problem, page 16) or as an appetizer.

¼ cup gochujang, or red pepper paste

¼ cup mayonnaise

2 tablespoons honey

1 tablespoon sesame oil

2 teaspoons minced garlic

1 tablespoon sugar

2 teaspoons ground ginger

3 pounds whole chicken wings

Olive oil spray

1 teaspoon salt

½ teaspoon freshly ground black pepper

DAIRY FREE, GLUTEN FREE, NUT FREE

1. In a large bowl, whisk the gochujang, mayonnaise, honey, sesame oil, garlic, sugar, and ginger. Set aside.

2. Insert the crisper plate into the basket and the basket into the unit. Preheat the unit by selecting AIR FRY, setting the temperature to 400°F, and setting the time to 3 minutes. Select START/STOP to begin.

3. To prepare the chicken wings, cut the wings in half. The meatier part is the drumette. Cut off and discard the wing tip from the flat part (or save the wing tips in the freezer to make chicken stock).

4. Once the unit is preheated, spray the crisper plate with olive oil. Working in batches, place half the chicken wings into the basket, spray them with olive oil, and sprinkle with the salt and pepper.

5. Select AIR FRY, set the temperature to 400°F, and set the time to 20 minutes. Select START/STOP to begin.

(continued)

Korean Chicken Wings *continued*

6. After 10 minutes, remove the basket, flip the wings, and spray them with more olive oil. Reinsert the basket to resume cooking.

7. Cook the wings to an internal temperature of 165°F, then transfer them to the bowl with the prepared sauce and toss to coat.

8. Repeat steps 4, 5, 6, and 7 for the remaining chicken wings.

9. Return the coated wings to the basket and air fry for 4 to 6 minutes more until the sauce has glazed the wings and the chicken is crisp. After 3 minutes, check the wings to make sure they aren't burning. Serve hot.

Per Serving (5 wings): Calories: 913; Total fat: 66g; Saturated fat: 15g; Cholesterol: 244mg; Sodium: 1,722mg; Carbohydrates: 23g; Fiber: 1g; Protein: 59g

INGREDIENT TIP: You can use frozen wings for this recipe. Just increase the cooking time by 10 minutes. You can also use your favorite dips like ranch or blue cheese dressing for these wings.

SUBSTITUTION TIP: If you can't find gochujang or red pepper paste, you can make a substitute: combine 1 tablespoon red pepper flakes with 2 teaspoons soy sauce, 1 teaspoon honey, and ¼ teaspoon salt.

Spicy Grilled Steak,
page 158

8

Beef, Pork, and Lamb

Spicy Grilled Steak

PREP TIME: 25 MINUTES / COOK TIME: 12 TO 18 MINUTES / SERVES 4 / 390°F / AIR FRY

This spicy steak gets its kick from chipotle peppers and red pepper flakes. It's very simple to make, and is delicious served with salsa, guacamole, and pita breads or naan.

2 tablespoons salsa

1 tablespoon minced chipotle pepper

1 tablespoon apple cider vinegar

1 teaspoon ground cumin

⅛ teaspoon freshly ground black pepper

⅛ teaspoon red pepper flakes

12 ounces sirloin tip steak, cut into 4 pieces and gently pounded to about ⅓ inch thick (see Tip)

Cooking oil spray

DAIRY FREE, GLUTEN FREE, NUT FREE

1. In a small bowl, thoroughly mix the salsa, chipotle pepper, vinegar, cumin, black pepper, and red pepper flakes. Rub this mixture into both sides of each steak piece. Let stand for 15 minutes at room temperature.

2. Insert the crisper plate into the basket and place the basket into the unit. Preheat the unit by selecting AIR FRY, setting the temperature to 390°F, and setting the time to 3 minutes. Select START/STOP to begin.

3. Once the unit is preheated, spray the crisper plate with cooking oil. Working in batches, place 2 steaks into the basket.

4. Select AIR FRY, set the temperature to 390°F, and set the time to 9 minutes. Select START/STOP to begin.

5. After about 6 minutes, check the steaks. If a food thermometer inserted into the meat registers at least 145°F, they are done. If not, resume cooking.

6. When the cooking is done, transfer the steaks to a clean plate and cover with aluminum foil to keep warm. Repeat steps 3, 4, and 5 with the remaining steaks.

7. Thinly slice the steaks against the grain and serve.

INGREDIENT TIP: Always read labels when you buy steaks. The leanest cuts of beef include sirloin tip steak, top round steak, and top sirloin steak.

Per Serving: Calories: 141; Total fat: 7g; Saturated fat: 2g; Cholesterol: 52mg; Sodium: 115mg; Carbohydrates: 1g; Fiber: <1g; Protein: 18g

Beef and Cheese Empanadas

PREP TIME: 15 MINUTES / COOK TIME: 25 MINUTES / SERVES 5 / 400°F / AIR FRY

Getting your protein in a convenient, flaky little pocket is always a special treat. When you serve these air-fried empanadas for dinner, your whole family will be on board. Loaded with beef and cheese, the leftovers make a great lunch on the run or enjoy one for a satisfying snack.

Cooking oil spray

2 garlic cloves, chopped

⅓ cup chopped green bell pepper

⅓ medium onion, chopped

8 ounces 93% lean ground beef

1 teaspoon hamburger seasoning

Salt

Freshly ground black pepper

15 empanada wrappers

1 cup shredded mozzarella cheese

1 cup shredded pepper Jack cheese

1 tablespoon butter

FAMILY FAVORITE, NUT FREE

1. Spray a skillet with the cooking oil and place it over medium-high heat. Add the garlic, green bell pepper, and onion. Cook until fragrant, about 2 minutes.

2. Add the ground beef to the skillet. Season it with the hamburger seasoning, salt, and pepper. Using a spatula or spoon, break up the beef into small pieces. Cook the beef for about 5 minutes until browned. Drain any excess fat.

3. Lay the empanada wrappers on a work surface.

4. Dip a basting brush in water. Glaze each wrapper along the edges with the wet brush. This will soften the crust and make it easier to roll. You can also dip your fingers in water to moisten the edges.

5. Scoop 2 to 3 tablespoons of the ground beef mixture onto each empanada wrapper. Sprinkle the mozzarella and pepper Jack cheeses over the beef.

6. Close the empanadas by folding the empanada wrapper in half over the filling. Using the back of a fork, press along the edges to seal.

7. Insert the crisper plate into the basket and the basket into the unit. Preheat the unit by selecting AIR FRY, setting the temperature to 400°F, and setting the time to 3 minutes. Select START/STOP to begin.

8. Once the unit is preheated, spray the crisper plate with cooking oil. Working in batches, place 7 or 8 empanadas into the basket. Spray each with cooking oil.

9. Select AIR FRY, set the temperature to 400°F, and set the time to 12 minutes. Select START/STOP to begin.

10. After 8 minutes, flip the empanadas and spray them with more cooking oil. Resume cooking.

11. When the cooking is complete, transfer the empanadas to a plate. For added flavor, top each hot empanada with a bit of butter and let melt. Repeat steps 8, 9, and 10 for the remaining empanadas.

12. Cool for 5 minutes before serving.

Per Serving: *Calories: 633; Total fat: 26g; Saturated fat: 14g; Cholesterol: 68mg; Sodium: 663mg; Carbohydrates: 73g; Fiber: <1g; Protein: 30g*

INGREDIENT TIP: Goya makes empanada wrappers called "discos" that are usually available in the freezer section of most grocery stores. If you can't find them, use egg roll wrappers instead.

Beef and Broccoli

PREP TIME: 10 MINUTES / COOK TIME: 15 TO 18 MINUTES / SERVES 4 / 400°F / AIR FRY

Beef and broccoli is a delicious and hearty Chinese dish that is usually made with lots of soy sauce and oyster sauce, which sends the sodium content through the roof. Mushrooms are used here instead; they add a meaty flavor that is a good substitute for those high-sodium ingredients.

2 tablespoons cornstarch

½ cup low-sodium beef broth

1 teaspoon low-sodium soy sauce

12 ounces sirloin strip steak, cut into 1-inch cubes

2½ cups broccoli florets

1 onion, chopped

1 cup sliced cremini mushrooms (see Tip)

1 tablespoon grated peeled fresh ginger

Cooked brown rice (optional), for serving

DAIRY FREE, FAMILY FAVORITE, FAST, NUT FREE

1. In a medium bowl, stir together the cornstarch, beef broth, and soy sauce until the cornstarch is completely dissolved.

2. Add the beef cubes and toss to coat. Let stand for 5 minutes at room temperature.

3. Insert the crisper plate into the basket and the basket into the unit. Preheat the unit by selecting AIR FRY, setting the temperature to 400°F, and setting the time to 3 minutes. Select START/STOP to begin.

4. Once the unit is preheated, use a slotted spoon to transfer the beef from the broth mixture into a medium metal bowl that fits into the basket. Reserve the broth. Add the broccoli, onion, mushrooms, and ginger to the beef. Place the bowl into the basket.

5. Select AIR FRY, set the temperature to 400°F, and set the time to 18 minutes. Select START/STOP to begin.

(continued)

Beef and Broccoli *continued*

6. After about 12 minutes, check the beef and broccoli. If a food thermometer inserted into the beef registers at least 145°F and the vegetables are tender, add the reserved broth and resume cooking for about 3 minutes until the sauce boils. If not, resume cooking for about 3 minutes before adding the reserved broth.

7. When the cooking is complete, serve immediately over hot cooked brown rice, if desired.

INGREDIENT TIP: Cremini mushrooms are baby portobello mushrooms. They are brown in color and have more flavor than white button mushrooms. Substitute button mushrooms if you can't find the cremini variety.

Per Serving: *Calories: 208; Fat: 5g; Saturated fat: 2g; Cholesterol: 49mg; Protein: 28g; Carbohydrates: 9g; Sodium: 122mg; Fiber: 2g; Sugar: 3g*

Meatballs in Spicy Tomato Sauce

PREP TIME: 10 MINUTES / COOK TIME: 15 MINUTES / SERVES 4 / 400°F / BAKE

These meatballs may become your air fryer go-to: You can make moist meatballs with a slightly crisp crust with much less effort than it takes making them on the stovetop. (And it's a great way to use up that leftover jarred pasta sauce I bet you have in your fridge right now!) To avoid smoke from the air fryer, use ground beef that is at least 95 percent lean.

3 scallions, minced

1 garlic clove, minced

1 egg yolk

¼ cup saltine cracker crumbs

Pinch salt

Freshly ground black pepper

1 pound 95% lean ground beef

Olive oil spray

1¼ cups any tomato pasta sauce (from a 16-ounce jar)

2 tablespoons Dijon mustard

DAIRY FREE, FAMILY FAVORITE, FAST, NUT FREE

1. In a large bowl, combine the scallions, garlic, egg yolk, cracker crumbs, salt, and pepper and mix well.

2. Add the ground beef and gently but thoroughly mix with your hands until combined. Form the meat mixture into 1½-inch round meatballs.

3. Insert the crisper plate into the basket and the basket into the unit. Preheat the unit by selecting BAKE, setting the temperature to 400°F, and setting the time to 3 minutes. Select START/STOP to begin.

4. Once the unit is preheated, spray the crisper plate with olive oil. Working in batches, spray the meatballs with olive oil and place them into the basket in a single layer, without touching.

5. Select BAKE, set the temperature to 400°F, and set the time to 11 minutes. Select START/STOP to begin.

6. When the cooking is complete, a food thermometer inserted into the meatballs should register 165°F. Transfer the meatballs to a 6-inch metal bowl.

7. Repeat steps 4, 5, and 6 with the remaining meatballs.

(continued)

Meatballs in Spicy Tomato Sauce *continued*

8. Top the meatballs with the pasta sauce and Dijon mustard, and mix gently. Place the bowl into the basket.

9. Select BAKE, set the temperature to 400°F, and set the time to 4 minutes. Select START/STOP to begin.

10. When the cooking is complete, serve hot.

Per Serving: *Calories: 360; Total fat: 12g; Saturated fat: 4g; Cholesterol: 154mg; Sodium: 875mg; Carbohydrates: 24g; Fiber: 3g; Protein: 39g*

SUBSTITUTION TIP: You can make these meatballs with lean ground pork or ground chicken or turkey or a combination of any of those meats. Just make sure you cook them until they register an internal temperature of 165°F for food safety reasons.

Taco Pizza

PREP TIME: 10 MINUTES / COOK TIME: 7 TO 9 MINUTES PER BATCH / SERVES 4 / 375°F / BAKE

You may be surprised to learn that pizza bakes beautifully—and quickly—in the air fryer! The crust crisps up, the cheese melts to perfection, and the toppings get hot and remain firm, not soggy. This recipe provides a spicy twist to a classic pizza pie.

¾ cup refried beans (from a 16-ounce can)

½ cup salsa

10 frozen precooked beef meatballs, thawed and sliced

1 jalapeño pepper, sliced

4 whole-wheat pita breads

1 cup shredded pepper Jack cheese

½ cup shredded Colby cheese

Cooking oil spray

⅓ cup sour cream

FAMILY FAVORITE, NUT FREE

SUBSTITUTION TIP: If you like, use cooked pork sausage, sliced chorizo, or precooked taco-seasoned ground beef in this recipe in place of the meatballs. Or add other vegetables, such as mushrooms, chopped onion, or chopped tomatoes, to the refried bean mixture. You can also use naan bread instead of the pita breads.

1. In a medium bowl, stir together the refried beans, salsa, meatballs, and jalapeño.

2. Insert the crisper plate into the basket and the basket into the unit. Preheat the unit by selecting BAKE, setting the temperature to 375°F, and setting the time to 3 minutes. Select START/STOP to begin.

3. Top the pitas with the refried bean mixture and sprinkle with the cheeses.

4. Once the unit is preheated, spray the crisper plate with cooking oil. Working in batches, place the pizzas into the basket. Select BAKE, set the temperature to 375°F, and set the time to 9 minutes. Select START/STOP to begin.

5. After about 7 minutes, check the pizzas. They are done when the cheese is melted and starts to brown. If not ready, resume cooking.

6. When the cooking is complete, top each pizza with a dollop of sour cream and serve warm.

Per Serving: Calories: 510; Total fat: 24g; Saturated fat: 12g; Cholesterol: 64mg; Sodium: 1,196mg; Carbohydrates: 50g; Fiber: 9g; Protein: 31g

Panko-Crusted Boneless Pork Chops

PREP TIME: 10 MINUTES / COOK TIME: 12 MINUTES / SERVES 4 / 400°F / AIR ROAST

In this quick recipe, juicy boneless pork chops are coated in a seasoned panko crust and air roasted until crispy and tender. Achieving this crunch with the air fryer is so much easier and faster than baking the conventional way. Pair this dish with sides of rice and asparagus or peas.

4 center-cut boneless pork chops, excess fat trimmed

¼ teaspoon salt

2 eggs

1½ cups panko bread crumbs

3 tablespoons grated Parmesan cheese

1½ teaspoons paprika

½ teaspoon granulated garlic

½ teaspoon onion powder

1 teaspoon chili powder

¼ teaspoon freshly ground black pepper

Olive oil spray

FAMILY FAVORITE, FAST, NUT FREE

1. Sprinkle the pork chops with salt on both sides and let them sit while you prepare the seasonings and egg wash.

2. In a shallow medium bowl, beat the eggs.

3. In another shallow medium bowl, stir together the panko, Parmesan cheese, paprika, granulated garlic, onion powder, chili powder, and pepper.

4. Dip the pork chops in the egg and in the panko mixture to coat. Firmly press the crumbs onto the chops.

5. Insert the crisper plate into the basket and the basket into the unit. Preheat the unit by selecting AIR ROAST, setting the temperature to 400°F, and setting the time to 3 minutes. Select START/STOP to begin.

6. Once the unit is preheated, spray the crisper plate with olive oil. Place the pork chops into the basket and spray them with olive oil.

7. Select AIR ROAST, set the temperature to 400°F, and set the time to 12 minutes. Select START/STOP to begin.

(continued)

Panko-Crusted Boneless Pork Chops *continued*

8. After 6 minutes, flip the pork chops and spray them with more olive oil. Resume cooking.

9. When the cooking is complete, the chops should be golden and crispy and a food thermometer should register 145°F. Serve immediately.

Per Serving *(1 pork chop): Calories: 352; Total fat: 9g; Saturated fat: 3g; Cholesterol: 151mg; Sodium: 527mg; Carbohydrates: 37g; Fiber: 2g; Protein: 32g*

SUBSTITUTION TIP: You can use many different herbs and spices to flavor these pork chops. Substitute 1 teaspoon dried thyme or oregano leaves for the chili powder. Or increase the chili powder to 2 teaspoons and add ½ teaspoon ground cumin.

Lemon Pork Tenderloin

PREP TIME: 5 MINUTES / COOK TIME: 10 MINUTES / SERVES 4 / 400°F / AIR ROAST

The tenderloin comes from a part on the animal near the rib cage that is rarely used, making it one of the most tender cuts of meat. It absorbs flavors readily and cooks quickly, which lets you put dinner on the table in mere minutes. Lemon tenderizes the pork even more and adds fabulous flavor.

1 (1-pound) pork tenderloin, cut into ½-inch-thick slices

1 tablespoon extra-virgin olive oil

1 tablespoon freshly squeezed lemon juice

1 tablespoon honey

½ teaspoon grated lemon zest

½ teaspoon dried marjoram leaves

Pinch salt

Freshly ground black pepper

Cooking oil spray

DAIRY FREE, FAMILY FAVORITE, FAST, GLUTEN FREE, NUT FREE

INGREDIENT TIP: You can often buy pre-marinated pork tenderloin in the supermarket, which makes this meal even faster to prepare. Just slice the pork and cook and you could eat in 10 minutes! Remember to always check the final temperature for food safety reasons.

1. Put the pork slices in a medium bowl.

2. In a small bowl, whisk the olive oil, lemon juice, honey, lemon zest, marjoram, salt, and pepper until combined. Pour this marinade over the tenderloin slices and gently massage with your hands to work it into the pork.

3. Insert the crisper plate into the basket and the basket into the unit. Preheat the unit by selecting AIR ROAST, setting the temperature to 400°F, and setting the time to 3 minutes. Select START/STOP to begin.

4. Once the unit is preheated, spray the crisper plate with cooking oil. Place the pork into the basket.

5. Select AIR ROAST, set the temperature to 400°F, and set the time to 10 minutes. Select START/STOP to begin.

6. When the cooking is complete, a food thermometer inserted into the pork should register at least 145°F. Let the pork stand for 5 minutes and serve.

Per Serving: *Calories: 209; Total fat: 8g; Saturated fat: 2g; Cholesterol: 83mg; Sodium: 104mg; Carbohydrates: 5g; Fiber: 0g; Protein: 30g*

Barbecued Baby Back Ribs

PREP TIME: 5 MINUTES, PLUS 30 MINUTES TO MARINATE / COOK TIME: 30 MINUTES /
SERVES 4 / 360°F / AIR ROAST

The air fryer is one of the best ways to prepare baby back ribs so they are tender and crisp with a mouthwatering sauce. This recipe is loaded with flavor, and your ribs will turn out finger-licking good! Plan on about 1½ pounds of ribs per person because of the bones. Grab your favorite barbecue sauce and dig in.

---

1 (6-pound) rack baby back ribs

1 teaspoon onion powder

1 teaspoon garlic powder

1 teaspoon light brown sugar

1 teaspoon dried oregano

Salt

Freshly ground black pepper

Cooking oil spray

½ cup barbecue sauce

DAIRY FREE, FAMILY FAVORITE, NUT FREE

1. Use a sharp knife to remove the thin membrane from the back of the ribs. Cut the rack in half, or as needed, so the ribs fit in the air fryer basket. The best way to do this is to cut the ribs into 4- or 5-rib sections.

2. In a small bowl, stir together the onion powder, garlic powder, brown sugar, and oregano and season with salt and pepper. Rub the spice seasoning onto the front and back of the ribs.

3. Cover the ribs with plastic wrap or foil and let sit at room temperature for 30 minutes.

4. Insert the crisper plate into the basket and the basket into the unit. Preheat the unit by selecting AIR ROAST, setting the temperature to 360°F, and setting the time to 3 minutes. Select START/STOP to begin.

5. Once the unit is preheated, spray the crisper plate with cooking oil. Place the ribs into the basket. It is okay to stack them.

6. Select AIR ROAST, set the temperature to 360°F, and set the time to 30 minutes. Select START/STOP to begin.

(continued)

Barbecued Baby Back Ribs *continued*

7. After 15 minutes, flip the ribs. Resume cooking for 15 minutes, or until a food thermometer registers 190°F.

8. When the cooking is complete, transfer the ribs to a serving dish. Drizzle the ribs with the barbecue sauce and serve.

Per Serving: *Calories: 375; Total fat: 27g; Saturated fat: 10g; Cholesterol: 90mg; Sodium: 474mg; Carbohydrates: 13g; Fiber: 1g; Protein: 18g*

SUBSTITUTION TIP: You can use a store-bought pork rub in place of the dry rub seasonings in this recipe.

VARIATION TIP: Make this a gluten-free recipe by using gluten-free barbecue sauce. Be sure to check the label.

Pork Teriyaki

PREP TIME: 10 MINUTES / COOK TIME: 13 MINUTES / SERVES 4 / 400°F / AIR ROAST

Pork tenderloin is a fabulous cut to cook in the air fryer. The meat has little fat, but still turns out tender and juicy. The recipe uses just a few simple ingredients you probably already have in the pantry. Use a store-bought teriyaki sauce or make your own. Either way, in less than 30 minutes, you will have a dinner on the table that the whole family will love.

1 head broccoli, trimmed into florets

1 tablespoon extra-virgin olive oil

¼ teaspoon sea salt

¼ teaspoon freshly ground black pepper

1 pound pork tenderloin, trimmed and cut into 1-inch pieces

½ cup teriyaki sauce, divided

Olive oil spray

2 cups cooked brown rice

Sesame seeds, for garnish

DAIRY FREE, FAMILY FAVORITE, FAST, NUT FREE

1. Insert the crisper plate into the basket and the basket into the unit. Preheat the unit by selecting AIR ROAST, setting the temperature to 400°F, and setting the time to 3 minutes. Select START/STOP to begin.

2. In a large bowl, toss together the broccoli, olive oil, salt, and pepper.

3. In a medium bowl, toss together the pork and 3 tablespoons of teriyaki sauce to coat the meat.

4. Once the unit is preheated, spray the crisper plate with olive oil. Put the broccoli and pork into the basket. Spray them with olive oil and drizzle with 1 tablespoon of teriyaki sauce.

5. Select AIR ROAST, set the temperature to 400°F, and set the time to 13 minutes. Select START/STOP to begin.

(continued)

Pork Teriyaki *continued*

6. After 10 to 12 minutes, the broccoli is tender and light golden brown and a food thermometer inserted into the pork should register 145°F. Remove the basket and drizzle the broccoli and pork with the remaining ¼ cup of teriyaki sauce and toss to coat. Reinsert the basket to resume cooking for 1 minute.

7. When the cooking is complete, serve immediately over the hot cooked rice, if desired, garnished with the sesame seeds.

SUBSTITUTION TIP: Use any fresh veggies you have in the crisper in place of the broccoli florets. Carrots, Brussels sprouts, or green beans would also work well in this recipe.

Per Serving: *Calories 332; Total fat: 7g; Saturated fat: 2g; Cholesterol: 45mg; Sodium: 1477mg; Carbohydrates: 35g; Fiber: 6g; Protein: 33g*

Greek Lamb Burgers

PREP TIME: 8 MINUTES / COOK TIME: 15 TO 18 MINUTES / SERVES 4 / 360°F / AIR FRY

This recipe is a way to think outside the traditional barbecue flavors when it comes to burgers. These lamb burgers, mixed with homemade Moroccan-style spice mix and garlic, are lean and delicious. Topped with homemade Greek dip and cucumber slices, this makes a great light lunch or dinner.

1 teaspoon ground ginger

½ teaspoon ground coriander

¼ teaspoon freshly ground white pepper

½ teaspoon ground cinnamon

½ teaspoon dried oregano

¼ teaspoon ground allspice

¼ teaspoon ground turmeric

½ cup low-fat plain Greek yogurt

1 pound ground lamb

1 teaspoon garlic paste

¼ teaspoon salt

¼ teaspoon freshly ground black pepper

Cooking oil spray

4 hamburger buns

½ cucumber, thinly sliced

FAST, NUT FREE

1. In a small bowl, stir together the ginger, coriander, white pepper, cinnamon, oregano, allspice, and turmeric.

2. Put the yogurt in a small bowl and add half the spice mixture. Mix well and refrigerate.

3. Insert the crisper plate into the basket and the basket into the unit. Preheat the unit by selecting AIR FRY, setting the temperature to 360°F, and setting the time to 3 minutes. Select START/STOP to begin.

4. In a large bowl, combine the lamb, garlic paste, remaining spice mix, salt, and pepper. Gently but thoroughly mix the ingredients with your hands. Form the meat into 4 patties.

5. Once the unit is preheated, spray the crisper plate with cooking oil, and place the patties into the basket.

6. Select AIR FRY, set the temperature to 360°F, and set the time to 18 minutes. Select START/STOP to begin.

7. After 15 minutes, check the burgers. If a food thermometer inserted into the burgers registers 160°F, the burgers are done. If not, resume cooking.

8. When the cooking is complete, assemble the burgers on the buns with cucumber slices and a dollop of the yogurt dip.

Per Serving *(1 burger): Calories: 475; Total fat: 30g; Saturated fat: 12g; Cholesterol: 87mg; Sodium: 513mg; Carbohydrates: 26g; Fiber: 1g; Protein: 26g*

SUBSTITUTION TIP: You can make this recipe using ground chicken, ground turkey, or ground beef. Just make sure the burgers are cooked to 165°F for ground poultry, and 160°F for ground beef, and measure that temperature with a food thermometer, for food safety reasons.

Marble Cheesecake,
page 182

9
Dessert

Marble Cheesecake

PREP TIME: 10 MINUTES / COOK TIME: 20 MINUTES / SERVES 8 / 325°F / BAKE

A cheesecake cooked in the air fryer seems improbable, but it works! This cheesecake is a combination of vanilla and chocolate. It's not only delicious, but it's gorgeous, too. Splurge and enjoy after a weeknight meal.

---

1 cup graham cracker crumbs

3 tablespoons butter, at room temperature

1½ (8-ounce) packages cream cheese, at room temperature

⅓ cup sugar

2 eggs, beaten

1 tablespoon all-purpose flour

1 teaspoon vanilla extract

¼ cup chocolate syrup

FAMILY FAVORITE, FAST, NUT FREE, VEGETARIAN

1. In a small bowl, stir together the graham cracker crumbs and butter. Press the crust into the bottom of a 6-by-2-inch round baking pan and freeze to set while you prepare the filling.

2. In a medium bowl, stir together the cream cheese and sugar until mixed well.

3. One at a time, beat in the eggs. Add the flour and vanilla and stir to combine.

4. Transfer ⅔ cup of filling to a small bowl and stir in the chocolate syrup until combined.

5. Insert the crisper plate into the basket and the basket into the unit. Preheat the unit by selecting BAKE, setting the temperature to 325°F, and setting the time to 3 minutes. Select START/STOP to begin.

6. Pour the vanilla filling into the pan with the crust. Drop the chocolate filling over the vanilla filling by the spoonful. With a clean butter knife stir the fillings in a zigzag pattern to marbleize them. Do not let the knife touch the crust.

7. Once the unit is preheated, place the pan into the basket.

8. Select BAKE, set the temperature to 325°F, and set the time to 20 minutes. Select START/STOP to begin.

9. When the cooking is done, the cheesecake should be just set. Cool on a wire rack for 1 hour. Refrigerate the cheesecake until firm before slicing.

Per Serving: *Calories: 311; Total fat: 21g; Saturated fat: 13g; Cholesterol: 99mg; Sodium: 272mg; Carbohydrates: 25g; Fiber: 1g; Protein: 6g*

SUBSTITUTION TIP: Using this basic recipe, you can make other cheesecake flavors. Add ½ cup chocolate syrup and don't divide the batter for a chocolate cheesecake. Omit the chocolate syrup and add about ⅓ cup of lemon curd for a lemon cheesecake.

Chocolate Peanut Butter Bread Pudding

PREP TIME: 10 MINUTES / COOK TIME: 10 TO 12 MINUTES / SERVES 4 / 325°F / BAKE

Bread pudding is the ultimate comfort food. The addition of chocolate and peanut butter gives it a subtle richness and intensifies the flavors. Serve with heavy whipped cream to double the indulgence.

Nonstick flour-infused baking spray

1 egg

1 egg yolk

¾ cup chocolate milk

2 tablespoons cocoa powder

3 tablespoons light brown sugar

3 tablespoons peanut butter

1 teaspoon vanilla extract

5 slices firm white bread, cubed

FAMILY FAVORITE, FAST, VEGETARIAN

SUBSTITUTION TIP: Use different types of bread. You could use cubed doughnuts or croissants or try a quick bread such as banana bread or peanut butter bread.

1. Spray a 6-by-2-inch round baking pan with the baking spray. Set aside.

2. In a medium bowl, whisk the egg, egg yolk, chocolate milk, cocoa powder, brown sugar, peanut butter, and vanilla until thoroughly combined. Stir in the bread cubes and let soak for 10 minutes. Spoon this mixture into the prepared pan.

3. Insert the crisper plate into the basket and the basket into the unit. Preheat the unit by selecting BAKE, setting the temperature to 325°F, and setting the time to 3 minutes. Select START/STOP to begin.

4. Once the unit is preheated, place the pan into the basket. Select BAKE, set the temperature to 325°F, and set the time to 12 minutes. Select START/STOP to begin.

5. Check the pudding after about 10 minutes. It is done when it is firm to the touch. If not, resume cooking.

6. When the cooking is complete, let the pudding cool for 5 minutes. Serve warm.

Per Serving: Calories: 263; Total fat: 11g; Saturated fat: 3g; Cholesterol: 98mg; Sodium: 223mg; Carbohydrates: 36g; Fiber: 2g; Protein: 10g

Pineapple Cream Cheese Wontons

PREP TIME: 15 MINUTES / COOK TIME: 15 TO 18 MINUTES PER BATCH / SERVES 5 / 390°F / AIR FRY

These delicious little dumplings are filled with a sweet and creamy filling. The wontons become crisp as they cook. You can serve these delightful treats on a pool of chocolate sauce if you'd like, or just eat them plain.

---

1 (8-ounce) package cream cheese
1 cup finely chopped fresh pineapple

20 wonton wrappers
Cooking oil spray

FAMILY FAVORITE, NUT FREE, VEGETARIAN

1. In a small microwave-safe bowl, heat the cream cheese in the microwave on high power for 20 seconds to soften.

2. In a medium bowl, stir together the cream cheese and pineapple until mixed well.

3. Lay out the wonton wrappers on a work surface. A clean table or large cutting board works well.

4. Spoon 1½ teaspoons of the cream cheese mixture onto each wrapper. Be careful not to overfill.

5. Fold each wrapper diagonally across to form a triangle. Bring the 2 bottom corners up toward each other. Do not close the wrapper yet. Bring up the 2 open sides and push out any air. Squeeze the open edges together to seal.

6. Insert the crisper plate into the basket and the basket into the unit. Preheat the unit by selecting AIR FRY, setting the temperature to 390°F, and setting the time to 3 minutes. Select START/STOP to begin.

7. Once the unit is preheated, spray the crisper plate with cooking oil. Place the wontons into the basket. You can work in batches or stack the wontons (see Air Fryer Tip). Spray the wontons with the cooking oil.

8. Select AIR FRY, set the temperature to 390°F, and set the time to 18 minutes. Select START/STOP to begin.

(continued)

Pineapple Cream Cheese Wontons *continued*

9. After 10 minutes, remove the basket, flip each wonton, and spray them with more oil. Reinsert the basket to resume cooking for 5 to 8 minutes more until the wontons are light golden brown and crisp.

10. If cooking in batches, remove the cooked wontons from the basket and repeat steps 7, 8, and 9 for the remaining wontons.

11. When the cooking is complete, cool for 5 minutes before serving.

Per Serving: *Calories: 137; Total fat: 9g; Saturated fat: 5g; Cholesterol: 27mg; Sodium: 164mg; Carbohydrates: 13g; Fiber: 1g; Protein: 4g*

SUBSTITUTION TIP: You can use canned, drained pineapple tidbits in this easy recipe. Or substitute another type of fruit. Canned pears or peaches would be good; just drain them well and chop into small pieces before you stir them into the cream cheese. The recipe works well with reduced-fat cream cheese. It keeps the calories and fat content low, making it a bit more waistline friendly, and the difference in taste is imperceptible!

COOKING TIP: Check on the wontons throughout the cooking process to ensure they do not overcook. The wontons have finished cooking when the color has reached a light golden brown. If the wontons overcook, the filling may leak.

AIR FRYER TIP: You can choose to stack the wontons or cook them in separate batches. The total cook time indicated is for one batch that is stacked. Although stacking them is quicker, preparing the wontons in batches works best. If you stack them, you may have a few that are really soft and break apart when you try to flip them over.

Honey-Roasted Pears with Ricotta

PREP TIME: 7 MINUTES / COOK TIME: 18 TO 23 MINUTES / SERVES 4 / 350°F / AIR ROAST

Roasted fruit tastes completely different than raw fruit. Here, roasting caramelizes the sugars in the pears, giving them a slightly smoky-toffee flavor. For this recipe, choose firm pears that give only slightly when pressed with your fingers. Leave the peel on so the pears hold their shape as they roast. You can leave the stem on half the pears for a pretty presentation. The ricotta cheese adds creamy smoothness to the slightly crisp pears.

2 large Bosc pears, halved lengthwise and seeded (see Tip)

3 tablespoons honey

1 tablespoon unsalted butter

½ teaspoon ground cinnamon

¼ cup walnuts, chopped

¼ cup part-skim ricotta cheese, divided

FAST, GLUTEN FREE, VEGETARIAN

1. Insert the crisper plate into the basket and the basket into the unit. Preheat the unit by selecting AIR ROAST, setting the temperature to 350°F, and setting the time to 3 minutes. Select START/STOP to begin.

2. In a 6-by-2-inch round pan, place the pears cut-side up.

3. In a small microwave-safe bowl, melt the honey, butter, and cinnamon. Brush this mixture over the cut sides of the pears. Pour 3 tablespoons of water around the pears in the pan.

4. Once the unit is preheated, place the pan into the basket.

5. Select AIR ROAST, set the temperature to 350°F, and set the time to 23 minutes. Select START/STOP to begin.

6. After about 18 minutes, check the pears. They should be tender when pierced with a fork and slightly crisp on the edges. If not, resume cooking.

(continued)

Honey-Roasted Pears with Ricotta *continued*

7. When the cooking is complete, baste the pears once with the liquid in the pan. Carefully remove the pears from the pan and place on a serving plate. Drizzle each with some liquid from the pan, sprinkle the walnuts on top, and serve with a spoonful of ricotta cheese.

Per Serving: Calories: 203; Total fat: 9g; Saturated fat: 3g; Cholesterol: 12 mg; Sodium: 20mg; Carbohydrates: 30g; Fiber: 4g; Protein: 4g

SUBSTITUTION TIP: Bosc pears are the best choice for this recipe because they are firm, even when ripe. You can use Anjou pears instead; they may take less time to cook. Make sure you buy pears that are firm but give slightly when pressed with a finger, and that have no soft spots.

Gooey Lemon Bars

PREP TIME: 15 MINUTES / COOK TIME: 25 MINUTES / SERVES 6 / 350°F / BAKE

These dangerously delectable treats come together quickly to create a lemon lover's dream dessert. If you don't love lemon, this probably isn't for you. There's something unbeatable about the combination of lemony tartness with just the right amount of sweetness.

¾ cup whole-wheat pastry flour

2 tablespoons confectioners' sugar

¼ cup butter, melted

½ cup granulated sugar

1 tablespoon packed grated lemon zest (see Tip)

¼ cup freshly squeezed lemon juice

⅛ teaspoon sea salt

¼ cup unsweetened plain applesauce

2 teaspoons cornstarch

¾ teaspoon baking powder

Cooking oil spray (sunflower, safflower, or refined coconut)

FAMILY FAVORITE, NUT FREE, VEGETARIAN

1. In a small bowl, stir together the flour, confectioners' sugar, and melted butter just until well combined. Place in the refrigerator.

2. In a medium bowl, stir together the granulated sugar, lemon zest and juice, salt, applesauce, cornstarch, and baking powder.

3. Insert the crisper plate into the basket and the basket into the unit. Preheat the unit by selecting BAKE, setting the temperature to 350°F, and setting the time to 3 minutes. Select START/STOP to begin.

4. Spray a 6-by-2-inch round pan lightly with cooking oil. Remove the crust mixture from the refrigerator and gently press it into the bottom of the prepared pan in an even layer.

5. Once the unit is preheated, place the pan into the basket.

6. Select BAKE, set the temperature to 350°F, and set the time to 25 minutes. Select START/STOP to begin.

(continued)

Gooey Lemon Bars *continued*

7. After 5 minutes, check the crust. It should be slightly firm to the touch. Remove the pan and spread the lemon filling over the crust. Reinsert the pan into the basket and resume baking for 18 to 20 minutes, or until the top is nicely browned.

8. When baking is complete, let cool for 30 minutes. Refrigerate to cool completely. Cut into pieces and serve.

Per Serving: *Calories: 207; Total fat: 8g; Saturated fat: 5g; Cholesterol: 21mg; Sodium: 104mg; Carbohydrates: 34g; Fiber: 2g; Protein: 2g*

COOKING TIP: Don't let the idea of zesting a lemon scare you away if it's new to you! All you'll need is a fine grater or Microplane. The most important thing to remember is to gently zest only the yellow outer peel of the lemon, because, if you zest the white part beneath, it will taste bitter—and you're going for tart here, not bitter.

Baked Apples

PREP TIME: 6 MINUTES / COOK TIME: 20 MINUTES / SERVES 4 / 350°F / BAKE

Warm baked apples loaded with cinnamon, brown sugar, nuts, and spices make the most delicious fall dessert. Take it up a notch and serve these with sweetened whipped cream on the side. You can use this same method with pears instead of apples or change the walnuts to pecans and add some raisins.

4 small Granny Smith apples
⅓ cup chopped walnuts
¼ cup light brown sugar
2 tablespoons butter, melted

1 teaspoon ground cinnamon
½ teaspoon ground nutmeg
½ cup water, or apple juice

FAMILY FAVORITE, FAST, GLUTEN FREE, VEGETARIAN

AIR FRYER TIP: The water is added to the bottom of the basin of the air fryer, under the basket. Then the fryer basket sits in the drawer and you place the baking dish with the apples into the basket. The water helps add a little humidity while baking.

1. Cut off the top third of the apples. Spoon out the core and some of the flesh and discard. Place the apples in a small air fryer baking pan.

2. Insert the crisper plate into the basket and the basket into the unit. Preheat the unit by selecting BAKE, setting the temperature to 350°F, and setting the time to 3 minutes. Select START/STOP to begin.

3. In a small bowl, stir together the walnuts, brown sugar, melted butter, cinnamon, and nutmeg. Spoon this mixture into the centers of the hollowed-out apples.

4. Once the unit is preheated, pour the water into the crisper plate. Place the baking pan into the basket.

5. Select BAKE, set the temperature to 350°F, and set the time to 20 minutes. Select START/STOP to begin.

6. When the cooking is complete, the apples should be bubbly and fork-tender.

Per Serving: Calories: 233; Total fat: 12g; Saturated fat: 4g; Cholesterol: 15mg; Sodium: 45mg; Carbohydrates: 36g; Fiber: 6g; Protein: 2g

Apple-Cinnamon Hand Pies

PREP TIME: 15 MINUTES / COOK TIME: 25 MINUTES / SERVES 8 / 400°F / AIR FRY

Replace your traditional slice of pie with these cute little handheld pastries. Any kind of apple will work for this warm and flaky cinnamon treat. These are best served warm with a scoop of vanilla ice cream.

2 apples, cored and diced
¼ cup honey
1 teaspoon ground cinnamon
1 teaspoon vanilla extract
⅛ teaspoon ground nutmeg

2 teaspoons cornstarch
1 teaspoon water
4 refrigerated piecrusts
Cooking oil spray

FAMILY FAVORITE, NUT
FREE, VEGETARIAN

1. Insert the crisper plate into the basket and the basket into the unit. Preheat the unit by selecting AIR FRY, setting the temperature to 400°F, and setting the time to 3 minutes. Select START/STOP to begin.

2. In a metal bowl that fits into the basket, stir together the apples, honey, cinnamon, vanilla, and nutmeg.

3. In a small bowl, whisk the cornstarch and water until the cornstarch dissolves.

4. Once the unit is preheated, place the metal bowl with the apples into the basket.

5. Select AIR FRY, set the temperature to 400°F, and set the time to 5 minutes. Select START/STOP to begin.

6. After 2 minutes, stir the apples. Resume cooking for 2 minutes.

7. Remove the bowl and stir the cornstarch mixture into the apples. Reinsert the metal bowl into the basket and resume cooking for about 30 seconds until the sauce thickens slightly.

8. When the cooking is complete, refrigerate the apples while you prepare the piecrust.

(continued)

Apple-Cinnamon Hand Pies *continued*

9. Cut each piecrust into 2 (4-inch) circles. You should have 8 circles of crust.

10. Lay the piecrusts on a work surface. Divide the apple filling among the piecrusts, mounding the mixture in the center of each round.

11. Fold each piecrust over so the top layer of crust is about an inch short of the bottom layer. (The edges should not meet.) Use the back of a fork to seal the edges.

12. Insert the crisper plate into the basket and the basket into the unit. Preheat the unit by selecting AIR FRY, setting the temperature to 400°F, and setting the time to 3 minutes. Select START/STOP to begin.

13. Once the unit is preheated, spray the crisper plate with cooking oil, line the basket with parchment paper, and spray it with cooking oil. Working in batches, place the hand pies into the basket in a single layer.

14. Select AIR FRY, set the temperature to 400°F, and set the time to 10 minutes. Select START/STOP to begin.

15. When the cooking is complete, let the hand pies cool for 5 minutes before removing from the basket.

16. Repeat steps 13, 14, and 15 with the remaining pies.

COOKING TIP: Check on the pies to monitor whether the cook time needs adjustment. The pies will turn golden brown when they are done. Handle them carefully while they're warm; they will be fragile until cool.

Per Serving: Calories: 493; Total fat: 21g; Saturated fat: 3g; Cholesterol: 0mg; Sodium: 410mg; Carbohydrates: 49g; Fiber: 2g; Protein: 3g

Easy Cherry Pie

PREP TIME: 15 MINUTES / COOK TIME: 35 MINUTES / SERVES 6 / 325°F / BAKE

Evoke some childhood nostalgia with this Easy Cherry Pie. With your air fryer, you can have light and flaky piecrust filled with sweet cherry filling without ever turning on your oven! Make it à la mode with a scoop of vanilla ice cream on the side.

All-purpose flour, for dusting

2 refrigerated piecrusts, at room temperature

1 (12.5-ounce) can cherry pie filling

1 egg

1 tablespoon water

1 tablespoon sugar

FAMILY FAVORITE, NUT FREE, VEGETARIAN

1. Dust a work surface with flour and place the piecrust on it. Roll out the piecrust. Invert a shallow air fryer baking pan, or your own pie pan that fits inside the air fryer basket, on top of the dough. Trim the dough around the pan, making your cut ½ inch wider than the pan itself.

2. Repeat with the second piecrust but make the cut the same size as or slightly smaller than the pan.

3. Put the larger crust in the bottom of the baking pan. Don't stretch the dough. Gently press it into the pan.

4. Spoon in enough cherry pie filling to fill the crust. Do not overfill.

5. Using a knife or pizza cutter, cut the second piecrust into 1-inch-wide strips. Weave the strips in a lattice pattern over the top of the cherry pie filling.

6. Insert the crisper plate into the basket and the basket into the unit. Preheat the unit by selecting BAKE, setting the temperature to 325°F, and setting the time to 3 minutes. Select START/STOP to begin.

7. In a small bowl, whisk the egg and water. Gently brush the egg wash over the top of the pie. Sprinkle with the sugar and cover the pie with aluminum foil.

(continued)

Easy Cherry Pie *continued*

8. Once the unit is preheated, place the pie into the basket.

9. Select BAKE, set the temperature to 325ºF, and set the time to 35 minutes. Select START/STOP to begin.

10. After 30 minutes, remove the foil and resume cooking for 3 to 5 minutes more. The finished pie should have a flaky golden brown crust and bubbling pie filling.

11. When the cooking is complete, serve warm. Refrigerate leftovers for a few days.

Per Serving: Calories: 302; Total fat: 15g; Saturated fat: 2g; Cholesterol: 27mg; Sodium: 294mg; Carbohydrates: 40g; Fiber: 1g; Protein: 3g

SUBSTITUTION TIP: You can replace the cherry pie filling with any other canned pie filling you like. If you're making an apple pie, sprinkle a little cinnamon and sugar over the top of the crust.

INGREDIENT TIP: Cut the leftover piecrust into fun shapes, sprinkle them with sugar and cinnamon, and bake in the air fryer at 350°F for 2 to 4 minutes, or until the crust is golden. If you have leftover pie filling, heat it in the microwave and serve over vanilla ice cream.

Strawberry-Rhubarb Crumble

PREP TIME: 10 MINUTES / COOK TIME: 12 TO 17 MINUTES / SERVES 6 / 375°F / BAKE

Strawberries and rhubarb are the fruits of spring. They are delicious combined in this dessert with a cinnamon-scented oatmeal streusel baked on top. This is wonderful served with ice cream melting into each warm bite.

1½ cups sliced fresh strawberries

¾ cup sliced rhubarb

⅓ cup granulated sugar

⅔ cup quick-cooking oatmeal

½ cup whole-wheat pastry flour, or all-purpose flour

¼ cup packed light brown sugar

½ teaspoon ground cinnamon

3 tablespoons unsalted butter, melted

FAMILY FAVORITE, FAST, NUT FREE, VEGETARIAN

INGREDIENT TIP: Did you know that rhubarb is technically a vegetable? It is very tart and needs some sugar to be palatable, but it is full of fiber and loaded with vitamin C.

1. Insert the crisper plate into the basket and the basket into the unit. Preheat the unit by selecting BAKE, setting the temperature to 375ºF, and setting the time to 3 minutes. Select START/STOP to begin.

2. In a 6-by-2-inch round metal baking pan, combine the strawberries, rhubarb, and granulated sugar.

3. In a medium bowl, stir together the oatmeal, flour, brown sugar, and cinnamon. Stir the melted butter into this mixture until crumbly. Sprinkle the crumble mixture over the fruit.

4. Once the unit is preheated, place the pan into the basket.

5. Select BAKE, set the temperature to 375ºF, and set the time to 17 minutes. Select START/STOP to begin.

6. After about 12 minutes, check the crumble. If the fruit is bubbling and the topping is golden brown, it is done. If not, resume cooking.

7. When the cooking is complete, serve warm.

Per Serving: *Calories: 213; Total fat: 7g; Saturated fat: 4g; Cholesterol: 15 mg; Sodium: 5mg; Carbohydrates: 41g; Fiber: 3g; Protein: 3g*

Big Chocolate Chip Cookie

PREP TIME: 7 MINUTES / COOK TIME: 9 MINUTES / SERVES 4 / 300°F / BAKE

Chocolate chip cookies are a perennial favorite for a reason. But have you ever made one that was 6 inches in diameter? This fun recipe makes one big cookie that serves four people. Everyone breaks off a piece to enjoy. This cookie is especially wonderful served warm.

3 tablespoons butter, at room temperature

⅓ cup plus 1 tablespoon light brown sugar

1 egg yolk

½ cup all-purpose flour

2 tablespoons ground white chocolate

¼ teaspoon baking soda

½ teaspoon vanilla extract

¾ cup semisweet chocolate chips

Nonstick flour-infused baking spray

FAMILY FAVORITE, FAST, NUT FREE, VEGETARIAN

1. In medium bowl, beat together the butter and brown sugar until fluffy. Stir in the egg yolk.

2. Add the flour, white chocolate, baking soda, and vanilla and mix well. Stir in the chocolate chips.

3. Line a 6-by-2-inch round baking pan with parchment paper. Spray the parchment paper with flour-infused baking spray.

4. Insert the crisper plate into the basket and the basket into the unit. Preheat the unit by selecting BAKE, setting the temperature to 300°F, and setting the time to 3 minutes. Select START/STOP to begin.

5. Spread the batter into the prepared pan, leaving a ½-inch border on all sides.

6. Once the unit is preheated, place the pan into the basket.

7. Select BAKE, set the temperature to 300°F, and set the time to 9 minutes. Select START/STOP to begin.

(continued)

Big Chocolate Chip Cookie *continued*

8. When the cooking is complete, the cookie should be light brown and just barely set. Remove the pan from the basket and let cool for 10 minutes. Remove the cookie from the pan, remove the parchment paper, and let cool completely on a wire rack.

Per Serving: *Calories: 309; Total fat: 22g; Saturated fat: 14g; Cholesterol: 84mg; Sodium: 178mg; Carbohydrates: 49g; Fiber: 2g; Protein: 5g*

SUBSTITUTION TIP: You can use other types of chips in this recipe. Try milk chocolate chips or butterscotch chips. Or add about ¼ cup chopped pecans or cashews when you stir in the chocolate chips—but then the recipe wouldn't be nut-free.

Air Fry Cooking Chart for the AF100 Series Ninja® Air Fryers

INGREDIENT	AMOUNT	PREPARATION	TOSS IN OIL	TEMP	COOK TIME
Vegetables					
Asparagus	1 bunch	Whole, stems trimmed	2 teaspoons	390°F	8 to 12 minutes
Beets	6 small or 4 large (about 2 pounds)	Whole	None	390°F	45 to 60 minutes
Bell peppers (for roasting)	4 peppers	Whole	None	400°F	25 to 30 minutes
Broccoli	1 head	Cut in 1-inch florets	1 tablespoon	390°F	10 to 12 minutes
Brussels sprouts	1 pound	Halved, stemmed	1 tablespoon	390°F	15 to 20 minutes
Butternut squash	1 to 1½ pounds	Cut in 1- to 2-inch pieces	1 tablespoon	390°F	20 to 25 minutes
Carrots	1 pound	Peeled, cut in ½-inch pieces	1 tablespoon	390°F	13 to 16 minutes
Cauliflower	1 head	Cut in 1-inch florets	2 tablespoons	390°F	15 to 20 minutes
Corn on the cob	4 ears	Whole ears, husked	1 tablespoon	390°F	12 to 15 minutes
Green beans	1 (12-ounce) bag	Trimmed	1 tablespoon	390°F	8 to 10 minutes
Kale (for chips)	6 cups, packed	Torn in pieces, stemmed	None	300°F	8 to 10 minutes
Mushrooms	8 ounces	Rinsed, quartered	1 tablespoon	390°F	7 to 9 minutes
Potatoes, russet	1½ pounds	Cut in 1-inch wedges	1 tablespoon	390°F	18 to 20 minutes

INGREDIENT	AMOUNT	PREPARATION	TOSS IN OIL	TEMP	COOK TIME
	1 pound	Hand-cut fries*, thin	½ to 3 tablespoons, canola	390°F	20 to 24 minutes
	1 pound	Hand-cut fries*, thick	½ to 3 tablespoons, canola	390°F	23 to 26 minutes
	4 whole (6 to 8 ounces each)	Pierced 3 times with a fork	None	390°F	30 to 35 minutes
Potatoes, sweet	1½ pounds	Cut in 1-inch chunks	1 tablespoon	390°F	15 to 20 minutes
	4 whole (6 to 8 ounces each)	Pierced 3 times with a fork	None	390°F	30 to 35 minutes
Zucchini	1 pound	Quartered lengthwise, then cut in 1-inch pieces	1 tablespoon	390°F	15 to 18 minutes
Poultry					
Chicken breasts	2 breasts (12 ounces to 1½ pounds each)	Bone in	Brushed with oil	375°F	25 to 35 minutes
	2 breasts (8 to 12 ounces each)	Boneless	Brushed with oil	375°F	18 to 22 minutes
Chicken thighs	4 thighs (6 to 10 ounces each)	Bone in	Brushed with oil	390°F	22 to 28 minutes
	4 thighs (4 to 8 ounces each)	Boneless	Brushed with oil	390°F	18 to 22 minutes
Chicken wings	2 pounds	Drumettes & flats	1 tablespoon	390°F	22 to 26 minutes
Fish & Seafood					
Crab cakes	2 cakes (6 to 8 ounces each)	None	Brushed with oil	350°F	12 to 15 minutes
Lobster tails	4 tails (3 to 4 ounces each)	Whole	None	375°F	5 to 8 minutes
Salmon fillets	2 fillets (4 ounces each)	None	Brushed with oil	390°F	10 to 13 minutes

INGREDIENT	AMOUNT	PREPARATION	TOSS IN OIL	TEMP	COOK TIME
Shrimp	16 large	Whole, peeled, tails on	1 tablespoon	390°F	7 to 10 minutes
Beef					
Burgers	4 (4-ounce) patties, 80% lean	1 inch thick	None	375°F	8 to 10 minutes
Steaks	2 steaks (8 ounces each)	Whole	None	390°F	10 to 20 minutes
Pork & Lamb					
Bacon	4 strips, halved crosswise	None	None	350°F	8 to 10 minutes
Pork chops	2 thick-cut, bone-in chops (10 to 12 ounces each)	Bone in	Brushed with oil	375°F	15 to 17 minutes
	4 boneless chops (8 ounces each)	Boneless	Brushed with oil	375°F	14 to 17 minutes
Pork tenderloins	2 tenderloins (1 to 1½ pounds each)	Whole	Brushed with oil	375°F	25 to 35 minutes
Sausages	4 sausages	Whole	None	390°F	8 to 10 minutes
Frozen Foods					
Chicken cutlets	5 cutlets	None	None	390°F	18 to 21 minutes
Chicken nuggets	1 (12-ounce) box	None	None	390°F	10 to 13 minutes
Fish fillets	1 box (6 fillets)	None	None	390°F	14 to 16 minutes
Fish sticks	18 fish sticks (11 ounces)	None	None	390°F	10 to 13 minutes
French fries	1 pound	None	None	350°F	20 to 25 minutes
	2 pounds	None	None	360°F	28 to 32 minutes

INGREDIENT	AMOUNT	PREPARATION	TOSS IN OIL	TEMP	COOK TIME
Mozzarella sticks	1 (11-ounce) box	None	None	375°F	8 to 10 minutes
Pot stickers	1 bag (24 ounces, 20 count)	None	None	390°F	12 to 14 minutes
Pizza rolls	1 bag (20 ounces, 40 count)	None	None	390°F	12 to 15 minutes
Popcorn shrimp	1 box (14 to 16 ounces)	None	None	390°F	9 to 11 minutes
Sweet potato fries, frozen	1 pound (20 ounces)	None	None	375°F	20 to 22 minutes
Tater tots	1 pound	None	None	360°F	18 to 22 minutes

*After cutting the potatoes, allow the fries to soak in cold water for at least 30 minutes to removed unnecessary starch. Pat the fries dry. The drier the fries, the better the results.

Dehydrate Chart for the AF100 Series Ninja® Air Fryers

INGREDIENTS	PREPARATION	TEMP	DEHYDRATE TIME
Fruits & Vegetables			
Apples	Cored, cut into ⅛-inch slices, rinsed in lemon water, patted dry	135°F	7 to 8 hours
Asparagus	Cut in 1-inch pieces, blanched	135°F	6 to 8 hours
Bananas	Peeled, cut in ⅜-inch slices	135°F	8 to 10 hours
Beets	Peeled, cut in ⅛-inch slices	135°F	6 to 8 hours
Eggplant	Peeled, cut in ¼-inch slices, blanched	135°F	6 to 8 hours

INGREDIENTS	PREPARATION	TEMP	DEHYDRATE TIME
Fresh herbs	Rinsed, patted dry, stemmed	135°F	4 hours
Ginger root	Cut in ⅜-inch slices	135°F	6 hours
Mangos	Peeled, cut in ⅜-inch slices, pitted	135°F	6 to 8 hours
Mushrooms	Cleaned with soft brush (do not wash)	135°F	6 to 8 hours
Pineapple	Peeled, cored, cut in ⅜- to ½-inch slices	135°F	6 to 8 hours
Strawberries	Halved or cut in ½-inch slices	135°F	6 to 8 hours
Tomatoes	Cut in ⅜-inch slices or grated; steam if planning to rehydrate	135°F	6 to 8 hours
Meat, Poultry, Fish			
Beef jerky	Cut in ¼-inch slices; marinate overnight	150°F	5 to 7 hours
Chicken jerky	Cut in ¼-inch slices; marinate overnight	150°F	5 to 7 hours
Salmon jerky	Cut in ¼-inch slices; marinate overnight	150°F	3 to 5 hours
Turkey jerky	Cut in ¼-inch slices; marinate overnight	150°F	5 to 7 hours

Air Fry Cooking Chart for the AF160 Series Ninja® Air Fryers

INGREDIENT	AMOUNT	PREPARATION	TOSS IN OIL	TEMP	COOK TIME
Vegetables					
Asparagus	2 bunches	Whole, stems trimmed	2 teaspoons	390°F	11 to 13 minutes
Beets	6 small or 4 large (about 2 pounds)	Whole	None	390°F	45 to 60 minutes
Bell peppers (for roasting)	4 peppers	Whole	None	400°F	26 to 30 minutes
Broccoli	1 head	Cut in 1-inch florets	1 tablespoon	390°F	13 to 16 minutes
Brussels sprouts	2 pounds	Halved, stemmed	1 tablespoon	390°F	18 to 22 minutes
Butternut squash	2 pounds	Cut in 1- to 2-inch pieces	1 tablespoon	390°F	23 to 26 minutes
Carrots	2 pounds	Peeled, cut in ½-inch pieces	1 tablespoon	400°F	20 to 24 minutes
Cauliflower	2 heads (about 2 pounds)	Cut in 1-inch florets	2 tablespoons	390°F	20 to 24 minutes
Corn on the cob	4 ears	Whole, husked	1 tablespoon	390°F	12 to 15 minutes
Green beans	2 bags (12 ounces each)	Trimmed	1 tablespoon	390°F	12 to 14 minutes
Kale (for chips)	½ bag (8 ounces)	Torn in pieces, stemmed	None	300°F	8 to 10 minutes
Mushrooms	2 packages (10 ounces each)	Rinsed, quartered	1 tablespoon	390°F	10 to 12 minutes
Potatoes, russet	2 pounds	Cut in 1-inch wedges	1 tablespoon	390°F	20 to 25 minutes
	1 pound	Hand-cut fries*, thin	½ to 3 tablespoons, canola	390°F	20 to 24 minutes

INGREDIENT	AMOUNT	PREPARATION	TOSS IN OIL	TEMP	COOK TIME
	2 pounds	Hand-cut fries*, thick	½ to 3 tablespoons, canola	390°F	23 to 26 minutes
	4 whole (6 to 8 ounces each)	Pierced 3 times with a fork	None	390°F	30 to 35 minutes
Potatoes, sweet	2 pounds	Cut in 1-inch chunks	1 tablespoon	390°F	20 to 24 minutes
	4 whole (6 to 8 ounces each)	Pierced 3 times with a fork	None	390°F	30 to 35 minutes
Zucchini	2 pounds	Quartered lengthwise, then cut in 1-inch pieces	1 tablespoon	390°F	18 to 20 minutes
Poultry					
Chicken breasts	2 breasts (12 ounces to 1½ pounds each)	Bone in	Brush with oil	375°F	25 to 35 minutes
	2 breasts (8 to 12 ounces each)	Boneless	Brush with oil	375°F	18 to 22 minutes
Chicken thighs	4 thighs (6 to 10 ounces each)	Bone in	Brush with oil	390°F	22 to 28 minutes
	4 thighs (4 to 8 ounces each)	Boneless	Brush with oil	390°F	18 to 22 minutes
Chicken wings	3 pounds	Drumettes & flats	1 tablespoon	390°F	22 to 26 minutes
Fish & Seafood					
Crab cakes	2 cakes (6 to 8 ounces each)	None	Brush with oil	350°F	12 to 15 minutes
Lobster tails	4 tails (3 to 4 ounces each)	Whole	None	375°F	5 to 8 minutes
Salmon fillets	2 fillets (4 ounces each)	None	Brush with oil	390°F	10 to 13 minutes
Shrimp	16 large	Whole, peeled, tails on	1 tablespoon	390°F	9 to 11 minutes

INGREDIENT	AMOUNT	PREPARATION	TOSS IN OIL	TEMP	COOK TIME
Beef					
Burgers	4 patties (4 ounces each), 80% lean	1 inch thick	None	375°F	8 to 10 minutes
Steaks	2 steaks (8 ounces each)	Whole	None	390°F	10 to 20 minutes
Pork & Lamb					
Bacon	4 strips, halved crosswise	None	None	350°F	8 to 10 minutes
Pork chops	2 thick-cut, bone-in chops (10 to 12 ounces each)	Bone in	Brush with oil	375°F	14 minutes
	4 boneless chops (8 ounces each)	Boneless	Brush with oil	375°F	14 to 17 minutes
Pork tenderloins	2 tenderloins (1 to 1½ pounds each)	Whole	Brush with oil	375°F	25 to 30 minutes
Sausages	6 sausages	Whole	None	390°F	8 to 10 minutes
Frozen Foods					
Chicken cutlets	5 cutlets	None	None	390°F	18 to 21 minutes
Chicken nuggets, precooked	2 pounds	None	None	390°F	15 to 18 minutes
Chicken nuggets, uncooked	3 boxes (12 ounces each)	None	None	390°F	20 to 22 minutes
Fish fillets	1 box (6 fillets)	None	None	390°F	14 to 16 minutes
Fish sticks	1 box (25 ounces)	None	None	390°F	12 to 14 minutes
French fries	1 pound	None	None	350°F	20 to 25 minutes
	2 pounds	None	None	360°F	28 to 32 minutes

INGREDIENT	AMOUNT	PREPARATION	TOSS IN OIL	TEMP	COOK TIME
Mozzarella sticks	2 boxes (12 ounces each)	None	None	375°F	9 to 10 minutes
Pizza rolls	2 pounds	None	None	390°F	14 to 16 minutes
Popcorn shrimp	2 boxes (14 to 16 ounces each)	None	None	390°F	14 to 15 minutes
Pot stickers	2 pounds	None	None	390°F	14 to 17 minutes
Sweet potato fries	1 pound	None	None	375°F	20 to 22 minutes
Tater tots	2 pounds	None	None	360°F	20 minutes

*After cutting the potatoes, allow the raw fries to soak in cold water for at least 30 minutes to remove unnecessary starch. Pat the fries dry. The drier the fries, the better the results.

Max Crisp Cooking Chart for the AF160 Series Ninja® Air Fryers

INGREDIENT	AMOUNT	PREPARATION	TOSS IN OIL	COOK TIME
Frozen Foods				
Chicken nuggets	1 box (12 ounces)	None	None	7 to 9 minutes
Chicken wings	2 pounds (32 ounces)	None	1 tablespoon	25 minutes
French fries	1 pound (16 ounces)	None	None	15 minutes
	2 pounds (32 ounces)	None	None	25 minutes
Mini corn dogs	14 ounces (20 to 24 count)	None	None	6 minutes

INGREDIENT	AMOUNT	PREPARATION	TOSS IN OIL	COOK TIME
	24 ounces (40 to 46 count)	None	None	8 to 10 minutes
Mozzarella sticks	24 ounces	None	None	6 to 8 minutes
Pizza rolls	1 bag (20 ounces, 40 count)	None	None	6 to 8 minutes
Pot stickers	24 ounces (20 to 24 count)	None	None	8 to 10 minutes

*NOTE: There is no temperature adjustment available or necessary when using the Max Crisp function.

Dehydrate Chart for the AF160 Series Ninja® Air Fryers

INGREDIENTS	PREPARATION	TEMP	DEHYDRATE TIME
Fruits & Vegetables			
Apples	Cut in ⅛-inch slices, cored, rinsed in lemon water, patted dry	135°F	7 to 8 hours
Asparagus	Cut in 1-inch pieces, blanched	135°F	6 to 8 hours
Bananas	Peel, cut in ⅜-inch slices	135°F	8 to 10 hours
Beets	Peel, cut in ⅛-inch slices	135°F	6 to 8 hours
Eggplant	Peel, cut in ¼-inch slices, blanched	135°F	6 to 8 hours
Fresh herbs	Rinsed, patted dry, stemmed	135°F	4 hours
Ginger root	Cut in ⅜-inch slices	135°F	6 hours

INGREDIENTS	PREPARATION	TEMP	DEHYDRATE TIME
Mangos	Peeled, cut in ⅜-inch slices, pitted	135°F	6 to 8 hours
Mushrooms	Cleaned with soft brush (do not wash)	135°F	6 to 8 hours
Pineapple	Peeled, cored, cut in ⅜- to ½-inch slices	135°F	6 to 8 hours
Strawberries	Halved or cut in ½-inch slices	135°F	6 to 8 hours
Tomatoes	Cut in ⅜-inch slices or grated; steamed if planning to rehydrate	135°F	6 to 8 hours
Meat, Poultry, Fish			
Beef jerky	Cut in ¼-inch slices; marinated overnight	150°F	5 to 7 hours
Chicken jerky	Cut in ¼-inch slices; marinated overnight	150°F	5 to 7 hours
Salmon jerky	Cut in ¼-inch slices; marinated overnight	150°F	3 to 5 hours
Turkey jerky	Cut in ¼-inch slices; marinated overnight	150°F	5 to 7 hours

BONUS NINJA
AIR FRYER 1-WEEK MEAL PLAN AND SHOPPING LIST

1-WEEK MEAL PLAN

To take full advantage of your Ninja Air Fryer, use it to cook breakfast, lunch, dinner—and even desserts and snacks, 7 days a week! Not sure how? Simply follow this one-week meal plan. Cut out the pages and take this along with the shopping list (see page 217) on your next visit to the grocery store and you'll be all set to air fry all the time! You can also download the meal plan and shopping list from www.CallistoMediaBooks.com/NinjaAirFryer.

Sunday
Breakfast: Fried Chicken and Waffles (page 39)
Lunch: Crab Cakes (page 116) and Crispy Broccoli (page 77)
Dinner: Chicken Cordon Bleu (page 145) and Savory Roasted Sweet Potatoes (page 85)
Dessert: Strawberry-Rhubarb Crumble (page 199)

Monday
Breakfast: Everything Bagels (page 31)
Lunch: Warm Chicken and Spinach Salad (page 121)
Snack: Nacho Kale Chips (page 81)
Dinner: Spicy Grilled Steak (page 158) and Glazed Carrots and Sweet Potatoes (page 88)

Tuesday
Breakfast: Mixed Berry Muffins (page 26)
Snack: Scotch Eggs (page 67)
Lunch: Chili Ranch Chicken Wings (page 133)
Dinner: Salmon on a Bed of Fennel and Carrot (page 96)

Wednesday

Breakfast: Blueberry Breakfast Cobbler (page 24)
Lunch: Beef and Cheese Empanadas (page 160)
Dinner: Spicy Air-Crisped Chicken and Potatoes (page 147)
Dessert: Big Chocolate Chip Cookie (page 201)

Thursday

Breakfast: Homemade Strawberry Breakfast Tarts (page 29)
Lunch: Taco Pizza (page 167)
Snack: Apple Chips (page 53)
Dinner: Beef and Broccoli (page 163)

Friday

Breakfast: Chocolate-Filled Doughnut Holes (page 36)
Lunch: Spicy Chicken Meatballs (page 123) and Panko-Breaded Mozzarella Sticks (page 64)
Dinner: Lemon Pork Tenderloin (page 171) and Fried Brussels Sprouts with Honey-Sriracha Sauce (page 83)
Dessert: Easy Cherry Pie (page 195)

Saturday

Breakfast: Puffed Egg Tarts (page 43) and Classic Hash Browns (page 37)
Lunch: Greek Lamb Burgers (page 178) and Roasted Corn on the Cob (page 87)
Dinner: Lemongrass Steamed Tuna (page 99)
Dessert: Honey-Roasted Pears with Ricotta (page 187)

SHOPPING LIST

Take this handy shopping list, organized by aisles in the grocery store, with you so you're sure to grab everything you need for the 1-week meal plan.

Produce

Apples (4)

Bell peppers, green (2)

Bell peppers, red (2)

Berries, mixed fresh (1 cup)

Blueberries (½ cup)

Broccoli (2 heads)

Brussels sprouts (1 pound)

Carrots (4 large)

Chipotle pepper (1)

Corn (4 ears)

Cucumber (1)

Fennel bulb (1)

Garlic (9 cloves)

Ginger, fresh (2-inch piece, or bottled; enough for 4 teaspoons)

Jalapeño peppers (2)

Kale (4 cups)

Lemongrass (1 stalk)

Lemons (5)

Mushrooms, cremini (1 cup sliced)

Onions, red (2)

Onions, white (3)

Orange (1)

Parsley (1 teaspoon)

Pears, Bosc (2)

Potatoes, russet (4)

Potatoes, sweet (3)

Potatoes, Yukon gold (4)

Rhubarb, sliced (¾ cup)

Spinach, baby (6 cups)

Strawberries, sliced (1½ cups)

Zucchini (1)

Dairy

Butter, salted (6 tablespoons)

Butter, unsalted (11 tablespoons)

Cheese, Cheddar, shredded (½ cup)

Cheese, Colby, shredded (½ cup)

Cheese, mozzarella, shredded (1 cup)

Cheese, mozzarella sticks (6)

Cheese, Parmesan, grated (¾ cup)

Cheese, pepper Jack, shredded (2 cups)

Cheese, ricotta (¼ cup)

Cheese, Swiss, grated (⅓ cup)

Eggs, large (19)

Milk, 2% (½ cup)

Milk, whole (⅔ cup)

Sour cream (1 cup)

Yogurt, plain Greek (1 cup)

Yogurt, vanilla (½ cup)

Meat, Poultry & Fish

Beef, ground, 93% lean (8 ounces)

Chicken breasts, boneless, skinless (7)

Chicken breasts, ground (1 pound)

Chicken sausage (1½ pounds)

Chicken thighs, bone-in, skin-on (4)

Chicken wings, whole (6 pounds)

Crabmeat, jumbo lump
(8 ounces)

Ham, chopped (¼ cup)

Lamb, ground (1 pound)

Salmon fillets (4)

Steak, sirloin tip
(1½ pounds)

Tuna steaks (4 small)

Canned & Bottled Goods

Baking spray, nonstick
flour-infused

Beef broth, low-sodium
(½ cup)

Honey (6 tablespoons)

Hot pepper sauce
(6½ teaspoons)

Maple syrup, pure

Mayonnaise (¼ cup)

Oil, extra-virgin olive
(9 tablespoons)

Oil, neutral such as coconut,
sunflower, safflower (⅓ cup)

Oil, sesame (2 teaspoons)

Olive oil spray

Refried beans (¾ cup)

Salsa (⅔ cup)

Soy sauce (7 teaspoons)

Sriracha (2 tablespoons)

Strawberry preserves
(½ cup)

Vinegar, apple cider
(3 tablespoons)

Vinegar, rice wine
(8 teaspoons)

Worcestershire sauce
(2 teaspoons)

Prepackaged & Frozen

Empanada wrappers (15)

Frozen puffed pastry
(⅓ sheet)

Hamburger buns (4)

Meatballs, beef,
precooked (10)

Pita, whole-wheat (4)

Refrigerated biscuits
(1 [8-count] can)

Refrigerated piecrusts (2)

Waffles, frozen (8)

Grains

Oatmeal, quick-cook
(⅔ cup)

Rice, brown (1 cup)

Pantry Items

Almonds, ground
(3 tablespoons)

Baking powder
(2¾ teaspoons)

Baking soda (¼ teaspoon)

Black pepper, freshly
ground

Bread crumbs (2 cups)

Bread crumbs, panko
(1½ cups)

Chocolate chips, semisweet
(16-ounce bag)

Chocolate,
white, ground
(2 tablespoons)

Cooking oil spray

Cornstarch (7 teaspoons)

Flour, all-purpose (4 cups)

Flour, self-rising (½ cup)

Flour, whole-wheat pastry
(1 cup)

Rainbow sprinkles

Salt

Salt, kosher

Salt, sea

Sugar, brown (1 cup)

Sugar, confectioners'
(½ cup)

Sugar, granulated (¾ cup)

Vanilla extract (1 teaspoon)

Walnuts, chopped (¼ cup)

Spices

Allspice, ground
(¼ teaspoon)

Chicken seasoning

Chili powder (1 tablespoon)

Cinnamon, ground
(1¾ teaspoons)

Coriander, ground
(½ teaspoon)

Cumin, ground
(2 teaspoons)

Curry powder (2 teaspoons)

Everything bagel spice mix

Garlic powder (2 teaspoons)

Garlic salt (½ teaspoon)

Ginger, ground (1 teaspoon)

Hamburger seasoning

Italian seasoning
(1 teaspoon)

Marjoram (1 teaspoon)

Mustard, dry (½ teaspoon)

Nacho cheese powder
(1 tablespoon)

Nutmeg, ground
(¼ teaspoon)

Old Bay seasoning
(1 tablespoon)

Onion powder (¼ teaspoon)

Oregano, dried
(2 teaspoons)

Paprika (2⅜ teaspoons)

Ranch salad
dressing mix
(1-ounce envelope)

Red pepper flakes
(⅛ teaspoon)

Tarragon leaves, dried
(1 teaspoon)

Thyme, dried (2 teaspoons)

Turmeric, ground
(¼ teaspoon)

White pepper, ground
(¼ teaspoon)

MEASUREMENT CONVERSIONS

VOLUME EQUIVALENTS (LIQUID)

US STANDARD	US STANDARD (OUNCES)	METRIC (APPROXIMATE)
2 tablespoons	1 fl. oz.	30 mL
¼ cup	2 fl. oz.	60 mL
½ cup	4 fl. oz.	120 mL
1 cup	8 fl. oz.	240 mL
1½ cups	12 fl. oz.	355 mL
2 cups or 1 pint	16 fl. oz.	475 mL
4 cups or 1 quart	32 fl. oz.	1 L
1 gallon	128 fl. oz.	4 L

OVEN TEMPERATURES

FAHRENHEIT (F)	CELSIUS (C) (APPROXIMATE)
250°	120°
300°	150°
325°	165°
350°	180°
375°	190°
400°	200°
425°	220°
450°	230°

VOLUME EQUIVALENTS (DRY)

US STANDARD	METRIC (APPROXIMATE)
⅛ teaspoon	0.5 mL
¼ teaspoon	1 mL
½ teaspoon	2 mL
¾ teaspoon	4 mL
1 teaspoon	5 mL
1 tablespoon	15 mL
¼ cup	59 mL
⅓ cup	79 mL
½ cup	118 mL
⅔ cup	156 mL
¾ cup	177 mL
1 cup	235 mL
2 cups or 1 pint	475 mL
3 cups	700 mL
4 cups or 1 quart	1 L

WEIGHT EQUIVALENTS

US STANDARD	METRIC (APPROXIMATE)
½ ounce	15 g
1 ounce	30 g
2 ounces	60 g
4 ounces	115 g
8 ounces	225 g
12 ounces	340 g
16 ounces or 1 pound	455 g

INDEX

ABOUT THE AUTHOR

 **Linda Larsen** is an author and home economist who has been developing recipes for years. She was the Busy Cooks Guide for About.com for 15 years, writing about how to cook, food safety, and quick cooking. She has written 39 cookbooks since 2005, including *The Complete Air Fryer Cookbook* and *The Complete Slow Cooking for Two Cookbook*, as well as *Eating Clean for Dummies*. Linda has worked for the Pillsbury Company since 1988, creating and testing recipes and working for the Pillsbury Bake-Off. She holds a BA in biology from St. Olaf College, and a BS with High Distinction in food science and nutrition from the University of Minnesota. She lives in Minnesota with her husband.

Printed in the USA
CPSIA information can be obtained
at www.ICGtesting.com
CBHW081240200224
4500CB00003B/14

9 781641 529563